IMAGES
of America

LAKE CHELAN
VALLEY

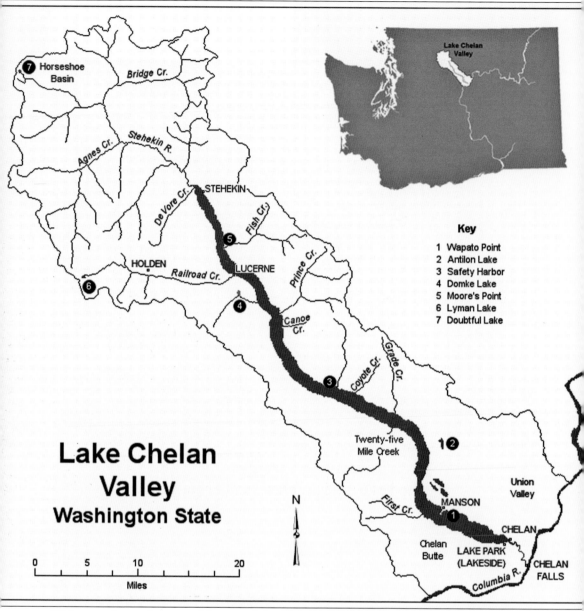

Lake Chelan Valley
Washington State

Key

1 Wapato Point
2 Antilon Lake
3 Safety Harbor
4 Domke Lake
5 Moore's Point
6 Lyman Lake
7 Doubtful Lake

This map shows the general layout of the Lake Chelan Valley with references to locations mentioned in the text.

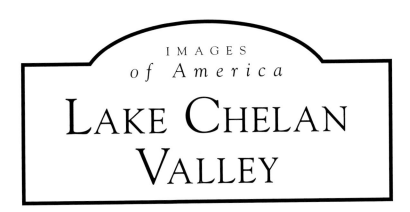

IMAGES
of America

LAKE CHELAN
VALLEY

Kristen J. Gregg and
the Lake Chelan Historical Society

ARCADIA
PUBLISHING

Published by Arcadia Publishing
Charleston SC, Chicago IL, Portsmouth NH, San Francisco CA

Printed in the United States of America

Library of Congress Control Number: 2008936541

For all general information contact Arcadia Publishing at:
Telephone 843-853-2070
Fax 843-853-0044
E-mail sales@arcadiapublishing.com
For customer service and orders:
Toll-Free 1-888-313-2665

Visit us on the Internet at www.arcadiapublishing.com

*To the early photographers of the Lake Chelan Valley, who left a
legacy of images for us to enjoy; to the memory of James Lindston,
founder of the society; and to all who have contributed time,
effort, and history to the Lake Chelan Historical Society.*

CONTENTS

ACKNOWLEDGMENTS

I would like to thank the following individuals from the Lake Chelan Historical Society for their support of this project: Dick Simonds, Linda Martinson, Ken Ross, Karen Lesmeister, Tom Kophs, Hobbie Morehead, Elizabeth Watson Perry, Don Lloyd, Mary Sherer, Concie Luna, Jane Lloyd, Marcelle Carpenter, Calli Eli, Roberta Simonds, and Dave Clouse.

In addition to the Lake Chelan Historical Society, a number of individuals and organizations provided material for this book. Christy Shearer and Kimberlee Craig from the Chelan County Public Utility District (PUD), Dennis King, Clint Campbell, the Oregon Historical Society, and the University of Washington Libraries Special Collections Division provided photographs and assistance.

My editor at Arcadia Publishing, Sarah Higginbotham, provided encouragement throughout the development of the book. It was a pleasure to work with her.

And finally, I thank my friends Tomomi, Ray, and the Medina family, and my parents, Carol and Tim, for their support and encouragement.

Unless otherwise noted, all images appear courtesy of the Lake Chelan Historical Society.

INTRODUCTION

Washington's largest lake, Lake Chelan, is one of the deepest lakes in the world. It occupies a glacially carved valley and extends over 50 miles from the mouth of the Stehekin River to its outlet, the Chelan River, which then drops over 350 feet in 3 miles where it meets the Columbia River. Besides the Stehekin River, which headwaters in the Cascade Range, other major tributaries to Lake Chelan are Railroad, Fish, Prince, and Twenty-Five Mile Creeks. The lake averages 1 mile wide and is walled by steep-sided cliffs along much of its length. To this day, the upper part of the lake is accessible only by boat, floatplane, helicopter, or hiking trail.

At the time of the arrival of Euro-Americans, several hundred people inhabited Chelan Indian villages, mostly on the north shore of the lake and along the nearby Columbia River. There was a seasonal shift to higher meadow locations in the summer months, where the families could graze and race horses. Although the permanent Chelan settlements were located within the valley, the normal hunting, fishing, and gathering range of the bands most certainly took them to a more extensive area, including the salmon fisheries of the Wenatchee Valley.

The earliest Euro-American explorers in the area were those establishing fur trading posts and searching for fur trade routes through the area. David Thompson conducted reconnaissance surveys for the Canadian North West Company between 1807 and 1811 and passed through the area in 1811. One of these explorers, Alexander Ross, wrote about spending a night in 1811 with friendly Native Americans who spoke of the lake "Tsillane," which means "deep water," the first mention of the word we now call "Chelan." Ross, in 1814, became the first documented Euro-American to cross the Cascade Range.

The Lake Chelan Valley remained unexplored by Euro-Americans until the 1870s, when trappers and prospectors entered the area. One theme was the search for routes through the Cascade Mountains for the fur trade. Another was the search for railroad routes. Daniel C. Linsley, the assistant chief engineer for the Northern Pacific Railroad, was sent in 1870 to evaluate routes across the North Cascades. Linsley crossed over a pass into the Agnes Creek drainage near the head of the Lake Chelan Valley. He noted that the route would require a tunnel over a mile long. To explore the other part of the route, he entered the Lake Chelan Valley from the Columbia River end and traveled up the lake to the Stehekin River and then to Agnes Creek, where he followed the valley up to the pass over to the Suiattle Valley. It was clear to all involved that the terrain was ill-suited for a railroad route. The accomplishment of the exploration was notable nonetheless.

In 1879, the Columbia Reservation was created on lands extending from Lake Chelan north to the Canadian border and from the Cascade ridge east to the Okanogan River. This reservation was intended to accommodate the Wenatchee, Entiat, Chelan, and Columbia tribes. Chief Moses (Quetalican) of the Columbia tribe, who often served as spokesperson for the group of tribes of the region, favored this arrangement. A U.S. military camp, Camp Chelan, was established at the lower end of Lake Chelan on the north side of the Chelan River. Other than the Chelans, who continued to live on their traditional lands, there was no large-scale settlement of the Native

Americans of the region on this reservation. In 1883, the government dissolved the Columbia Reservation and convinced Moses and the other leaders to cede the entire reservation in exchange for either residence on the Colville Reservation (which was established by executive order, not by treaty, in 1872) or 640-acre allotments in the former reservation area. This "Moses Agreement" was ratified by Congress in 1884. The Entiats were the only band to actively claim their allotments, settling on prime lands on the north shore of Lake Chelan. Several Chelan Indian families continued to live on their traditional lands without applying for allotments.

On May 1, 1886, the Lake Chelan Valley was opened to homesteaders. Ignatius A. Navarre with his wife and baby daughter arrived in April or May 1886. William Sanders and Henry Domke (also Dumpkey and Dumky) were prospectors who arrived over the mountains from the Methow Valley, with several misadventures along the way, in the same year. By 1888, homesteaders had claimed most of the available lakeshore land and settlement was moving into the higher elevations.

Early residents L. H. Woodin and A. F. Nichols established the area's first sawmill on the lake just south of the Chelan River at Lake Park—now known as Lakeside. They added a bunkhouse for the workers, which later became Darnell's Hotel, and a company store, which became Hardenburg's General Store.

Prospecting was a seasonal activity that flourished after M. M. Kingman and A. M. Pershall discovered viable ore deposits in the Horseshoe Basin above Stehekin and sold their claims for $30,000 in 1891. Henry Holden discovered the Holden Mine in the Railroad Creek area in 1896. Full-blown production did not start there until 1937. At the mine's peak, it had a payroll of over 400 workers, many of whom brought their families to the company town built by Howe Sound Company, the owner of the mine at the time.

Steamers played an important role in the history of the valley. Steamers on the Columbia River provided early links to larger communities downstream. Steamers on the lake itself linked communities and allowed people and goods to be transported between areas where road construction was impossible.

Rail transportation reached Wenatchee in 1892, but it was not until 1914 that a branch railroad line reached Chelan Falls.

The early homesteaders used ingenuity and hard work to develop irrigation systems for their fruit and vegetable crops with spectacular results. The Wapato Irrigation Company identified thousands of acres of land on the north side of the lake that were deemed irrigable and suitable for development. Much of the land that the company sought was in Native American land allotments, which could not be sold. It took an act of Congress to allow the Native American families to sell part of their holdings to the company. Eventually the company acquired 6,500 acres, and the area became the heart of Washington's apple production.

The valley experienced a dramatic change in 1927 with the completion of a dam at the base of the lake. The resulting 21-foot increase in the lake level flooded most of Lakeside as well as the grounds of the Field Hotel in Stehekin. The downtown of Manson was relocated up the hill, and Peter Wapato's dance hall site on Wapato Point ended up underwater.

The stories contained on these pages touch the highlights of Lake Chelan Valley history through the 1950s. The reader is encouraged to consult the books and articles listed in the bibliography to pursue the details.

One

THE EARLIEST RESIDENTS

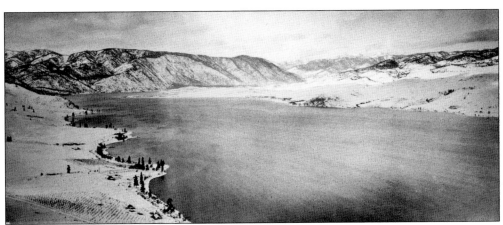

The attractiveness of the Lake Chelan Valley to the prospective settlers of the 1880s is apparent in this early up-lake view from Chelan Butte. Wapato Point, a peninsula extending into the lake (visible in this photograph), contained the largest flat expanse of land, but the relatively gentle slopes along the lake were prime locations for farming and ranching. These were also the areas of traditional occupation by the Chelan Indians.

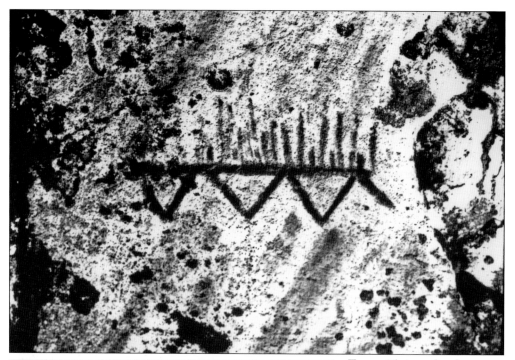

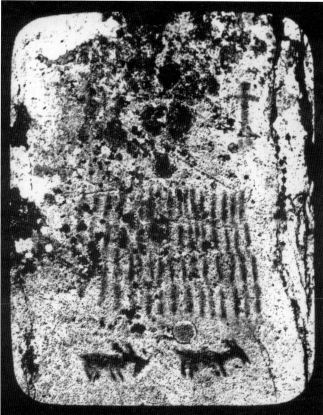

Ten to 15 sites of early Chelan villages, some year-round and some seasonal, have been located in the valley. The village sites were found from the base of the lake, near present-day Chelan, to the Grade Creek area, mostly along the north shore of the lake. Petroglyphs such as these have been found on the cliffs that border the lake. Many are now underwater as a result of the change in lake level after the completion of the dam in 1928. By 1870, a census conducted by the Indian agent for the region reported that the population of the Chelans, the Methows to the north, and the Entiats to the south was approximately 300. At that time, all were living on farms.

Chief Moses (Quetalican) was the leader of the Columbia Indians and served as a spokesperson and negotiator for several tribes, including the Wenatchi, Entiats, Chelans, Methows, and Okanogans. In 1879, he traveled to Washington, D.C., and as a result of meetings with government officials, a new reservation—the Columbia Reservation, also known as the "Moses Reservation"—was created. The reservation extended from Lake Chelan on the south to the Canadian border on the north and from the Cascade crest in the west to the Okanogan River and Columbia River in the east. Very few families relocated to the reservation, and it was returned to public domain in 1883. Native American families were given the choice of settling on 640-acre allotments within the boundaries of the former reservation or relocation to the Colville Reservation.

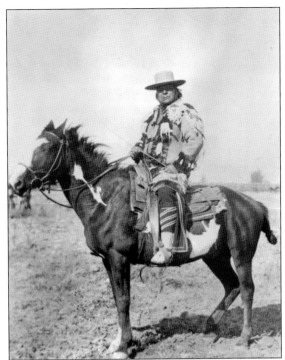

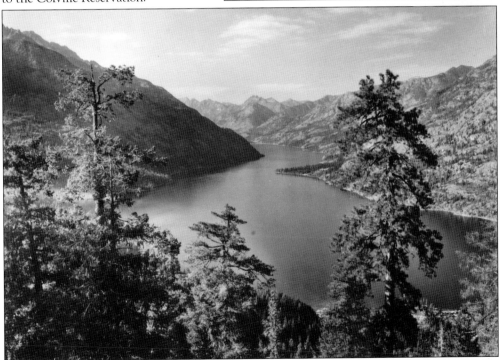

The earliest Euro-American settlers in the area were Henry Domke (also Dumpkey and other variations) and William Sanders, who arrived in the area in 1886. Domke Mountain, Domke Lake, and Domke Falls were named after Domke. This view toward the head of the lake was taken from the trail up to Domke Lake. The point of land extending into the lake is Moore's Point.

11

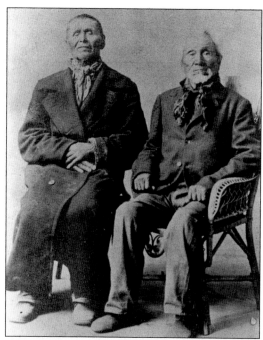

Wapato John (Nequiliken) is shown here (on the left) with his older half-brother Shilhohsaskt. John was born to Ken-em-tiq't and Que-til-qua-soon of the Entiat tribe. As a young man, Nequiliken helped his father run pack trains, and he worked in the Portland area as a longshoreman and as a cook. He and his wife, Madeline, operated a ranch and trading post in the Entiat Valley on the Columbia River before taking an allotment in the Mill Bay area near Manson. Wapato John had a reputation for fairness and was a highly respected member of the community.

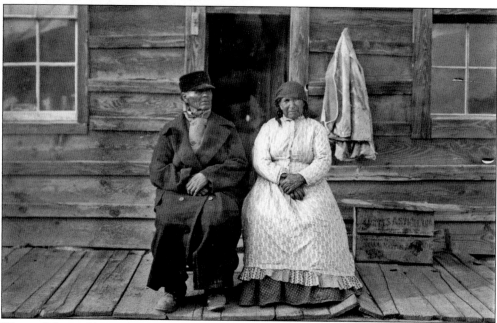

Wapato John and his wife, Madeline (Mee-mee-hulks), are shown in this photograph. Their five children who reached adulthood all ended up taking up allotments on or near the north shore of Lake Chelan. These included Peter (Que-til-qua-soon), Sylvester (Ke-up-kin or Celesta), Mary (who married Louis Ustah), Ann Mary (Tan-te-ak-o or Isadore, who married Johnny Abraham), and Charles (who married Matilda). At the time of the 1870 census, while living in the Entiat Valley, Wapato John had "4 head of Cattle, 9 Horses, 6 Hogs, 100 Chickens; 12 acres fenced and cultivated in Potatoes, Peas, Corn, Garden Seeds, and Apple Trees," and that he had "12 Log Cabins, 1 Store Room, 1 Barn and Stable."

Peter Wapato, Wapato John's son, claimed as his allotment the land in the Manson area that includes Wapato Point on the north shore of the lake about 7 miles up-lake from Chelan. He built a horseracing track with a grandstand and a dance hall on Wapato Point. People from all over the region came to Wapato Point to enjoy four- to five-day celebrations with horseracing, gambling, and dancing. Before the Manson High School had a football field, the school's football games were played at Wapato Point. Peter's wife was Hyacinth (Yacinda).

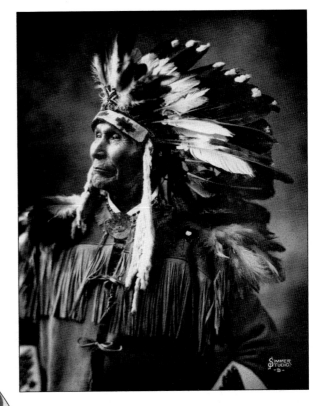

Long Jim assumed leadership of the Chelan Indians after the death of his father, Innomeseecha. After the Moses Agreement, many Chelan Indians moved to the Colville Reservation, but a few families stayed in their established homes and farms in the Chelan area without formally applying for allotments. Long Jim was one of the Chelan who stayed in the area and successfully made the case that he should be allowed to stay on the land where he and his family had been living and farming for many years. Long Jim later moved to the Colville Reservation.

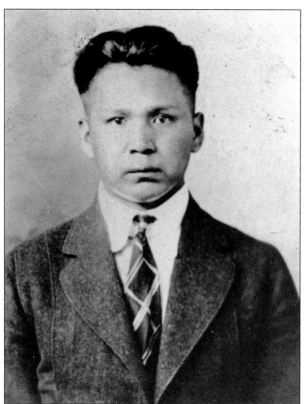

Paschal Sherman was born in Chelan in 1895 to Charlie and Matilda Wapato. He was known as Frank Wapato until he attended school at St. Mary's Mission in Omak, where he and his brother Paul were sent after the death of their father. He excelled academically and received a bachelor's degree from St. Martin's College after two years of study there. He went on to earn several additional degrees, including a doctorate and a law degree, and had an illustrious career as an attorney with the federal government. Paschal Sherman Indian School near Omak is named in his honor.

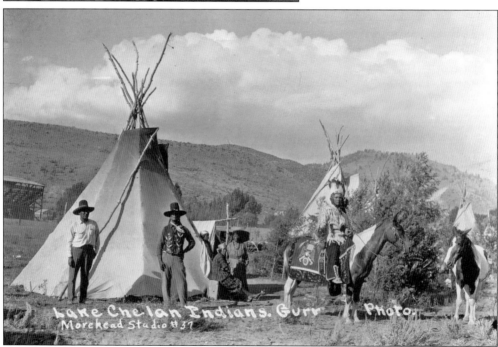

From left to right, Ed Walsh, Long Jim, Mrs. Ed Walsh, Mrs. Matthew Bill, Mrs. Bill Carden, and Matthew Bill gather in Chelan.

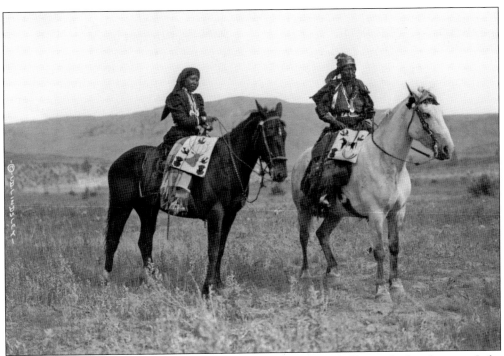

Matilda Wapato (right) and a young Okanogan woman with beaded bags ride their horses at Lake Chelan in this photograph taken by Edward Latham around 1910. (University of Washington Libraries Special Collections, NA1037.)

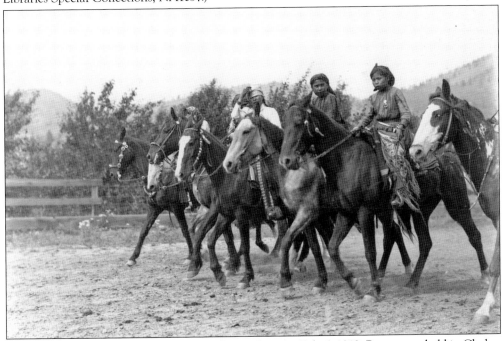

These young women were returning home after the races July 6, 1912. Races were held in Chelan at the Long Jim Track and at Peter Wapato's property on Wapato Point. (University of Washington Libraries Special Collections, NA1036.)

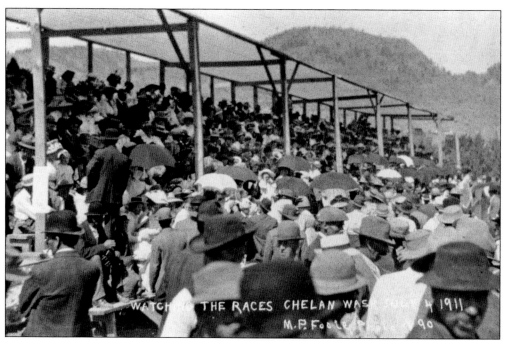

WATCHING THE RACES CHELAN WASH JULY 4 1911
M. P. FOOLE 90

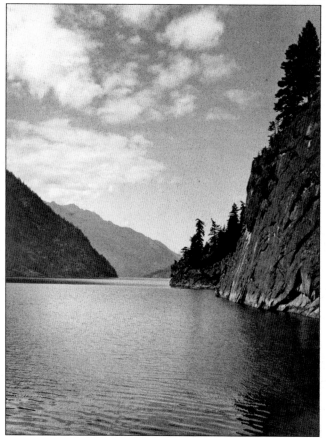

On Sunday afternoons, the grandstand overflowed as spectators watched their favorite horses race at the Long Jim Track in Chelan. The Fourth of July celebration was the occasion for several days of horseracing and other festivities in Chelan. Some 3,000 people attended Fourth of July horse races in 1901. This is a July 4, 1911, photograph.

"The Narrows" is a constriction of the lake separating the Wapato Basin from the Lucerne Basin. The Wapato Basin, which extends from the Manson area down-lake to Chelan and the mouth of the lake, has a maximum depth of about 400 feet. The Lucerne Basin, up-lake from the Narrows, has a maximum depth of 1,486 feet. At the Narrows, a shallow sill separates the two basins. Water depth there is a mere 127 feet.

Two

EARLY LOGGING AND MINING

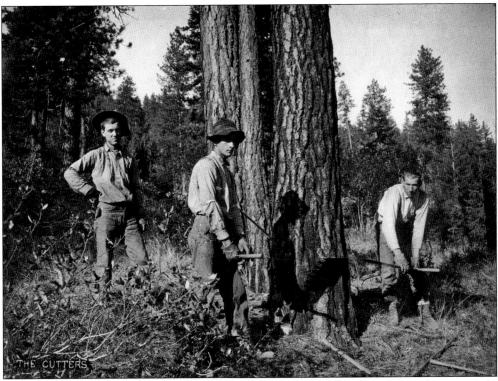

A timber supply was key to the expansion of settlement in the valley. Here Everett Province (left) and two other loggers are shown cutting timber in the Union Valley. Two-man saws or axes were used to cut the undercut in the large trees. The saw's cutting teeth and racker teeth can be seen as a shadow on the tree trunk. The cutting teeth sliced the wood on each side of the saw's kerf, while the racker teeth would remove the wood from the kerf. A properly sharpened saw could cut rapidly through these large trunks and would create a pile of worm-shaped cuttings at the base of the tree. The elevation range within Lake Chelan Valley gives rise to diverse forest types and species. Huge ponderosa pine trees grew at the lower to moderate elevations, while Douglas fir, true fir, and spruce were dominant at the higher elevations.

A second cut—the back cut—on the opposite side of the tree would finish the job. The fellers would move back quickly to avoid "widow-makers"—large, heavy dead limbs that could break off and injure or kill fellers. A tree is being felled in this 1908 logging scene.

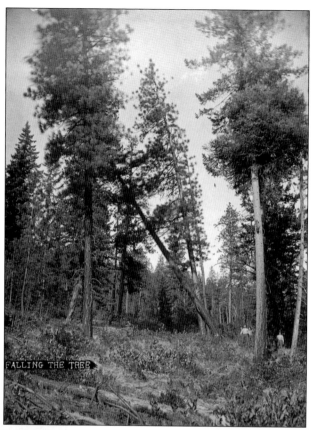

FALLING THE TREE

After trees were felled, their trunks were "bucked" into shorter sections, usually with one-man bucking saws. These logs were then "skidded" or dragged to a central landing area using teams of horses. "High grading"—taking only the largest or best trees—was common in the early days of logging.

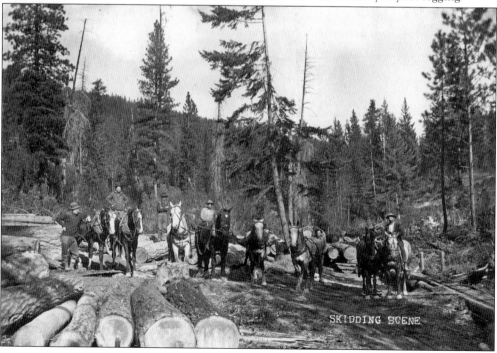

SKIDDING SCENE

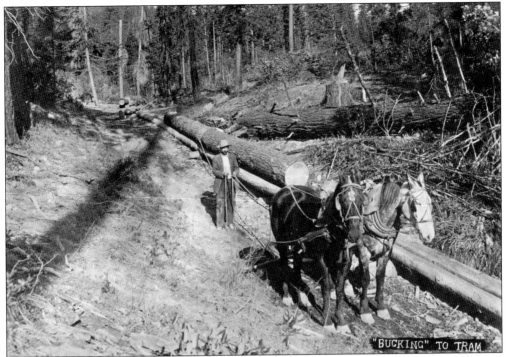

"BUCKING" TO TRAM

Logs were moved from the landing using a skid road or, in this case, a trough formed by two parallel logs. This is a scene at the Coyote Creek logging operation in 1908.

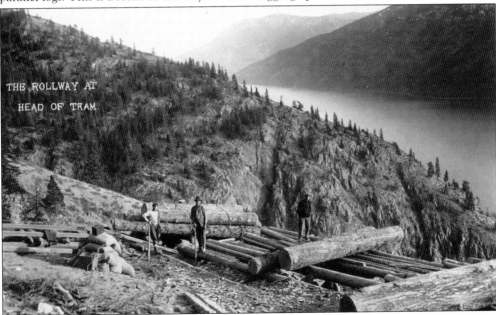

THE ROLLWAY AT
HEAD OF TRAM

The rollway at the head of the Coyote Creek tram is shown in this 1908–1909 photograph. Logs were stored at a log deck high above the lake, then rolled and chained onto a tram car. A pole with a cant hook on the end was used to move and control the large, heavy logs. Joseph Peavey, an East Coast blacksmith, added a spike to the end of this tool, and the "peavey" became the common tool throughout the logging industry for handling logs.

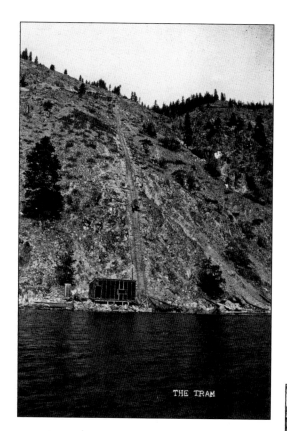

THE TRAM

Shown here is the loaded tram car being lowered on a steel and wood rail, using a cable controlled by an engine at the top of the slope. Once the logs reached the lake, they were tied together and rafted down the lake to a sawmill.

This scene—at "Painted Rocks" on the south shore of the lake near Stehekin—shows the type of terrain that early loggers and miners contended with in working in the upper reaches of the valley.

LAKE CHELAN AT PAINTED ROCKS 913

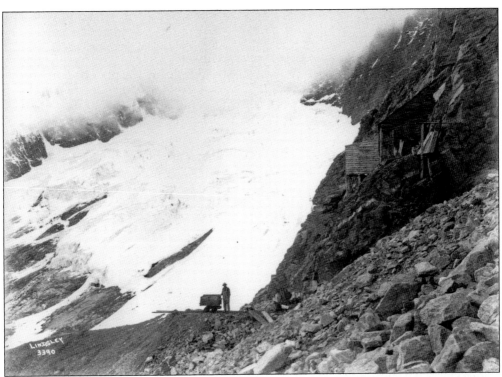

The Davenport mine was located by Morrison M. Kingman and Lloyd Pershall, his brother-in-law, in 1891. It is situated in Horseshoe Basin, a high cirque at the upper reaches of the Stehekin Valley. The mine operated during 1907 and 1908 under the Cascade Copper Company and around 1949 by the Horseshoe Basin Mining and Development Company. The mine consisted of over 500 feet of tunnel and produced lead, copper, silver, and gold. Mr. Beidler is shown in these photographs taken in 1911.

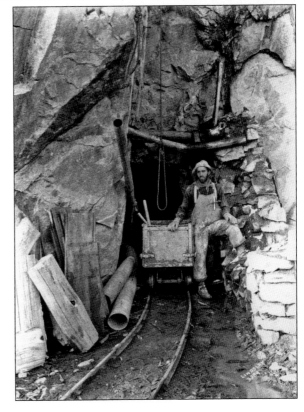

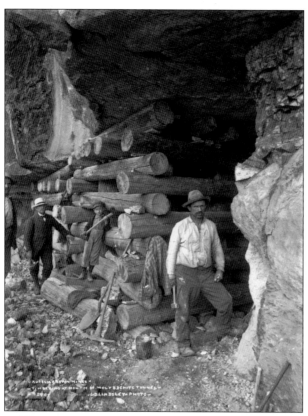

A supply of logs was important in mining. Timbering at the molybdenite tunnel of the Aurelia Crown Mine is shown in this 1909 photograph.

The crew of the Holden Mine is shown in this photograph taken on August 20, 1909. Crewmembers include Grover Kelly, George Clark, and the Faletto brothers: August, John, and Servine.

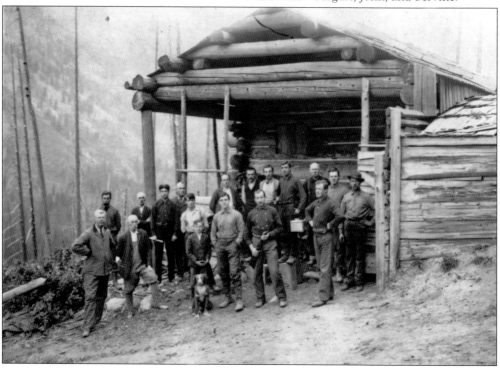

Two miners pose for photographer Lawrence D. Lindsley as they stand at the top of a tailing pile at a mine entrance.

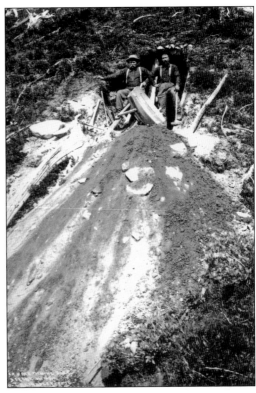

This view of prospector Jim Scheuyaulle's cabin in February 1907 shows why mining in the high country was a seasonal activity.

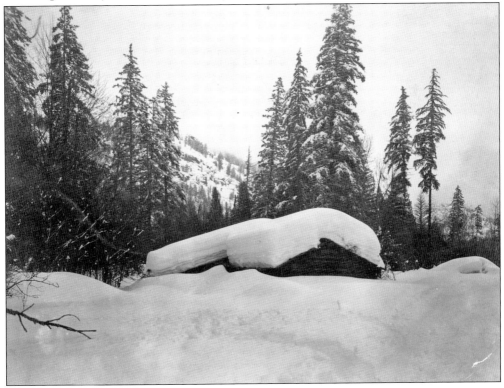

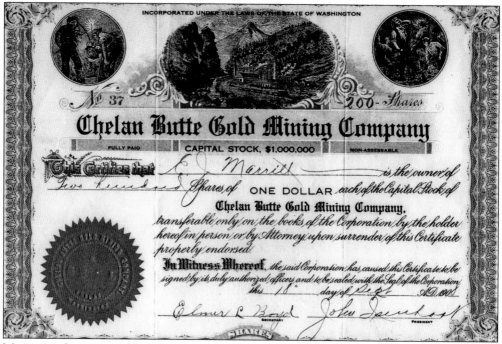

INCORPORATED UNDER THE LAWS OF THE STATE OF WASHINGTON

Nº 37   200 Shares

Chelan Butte Gold Mining Company

FULLY PAID   CAPITAL STOCK, $1,000,000   NON-ASSESSABLE

This Certifies that *E J Marritt* is the owner of *Five hundred* Shares of ONE DOLLAR each of the Capital Stock of **Chelan Butte Gold Mining Company**, transferable only on the books of the Corporation by the holder hereof in person or by Attorney upon surrender of this Certificate properly endorsed.

In Witness Whereof, the said Corporation has caused this Certificate to be signed by its duly authorized officers and to be sealed with the Seal of the Corporation this *18* day of *Sept* A.D. *1908*

Elmer L Boyd   *John Isenhart*
SECRETARY   PRESIDENT

Mining exploration of Chelan Butte started in 1906. In April 1907, gold float was discovered by S. Fourtner, who staked the first gold claim. Within weeks, the gold rush was on. Morris M. Kingman and A. M. Pershall, who had mined successfully in the Horseshoe Basin, rushed to the area and staked claims. Two of their Chelan Butte mining claims sold for $20,000 in June 1908. In July 1908, Kingman and Pershall formed the Chelan Butte Gold Mining Company and were selling shares.

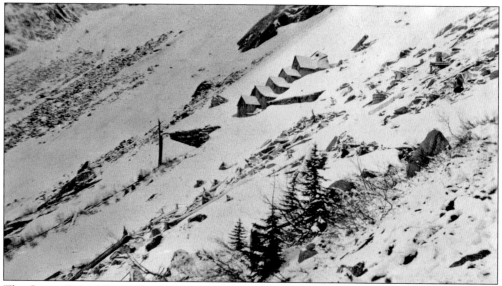

The Crown Point Mine is located in a cirque at the head of Railroad Creek, above Holden. The mine was operated by various owners from 1909 to 1924. There are more than 400 feet of drifts (horizontal shafts) at this mine. Almost 25 tons of molybdenite were shipped from the mine, in spite of its difficult location.

Three

CHELAN FALLS

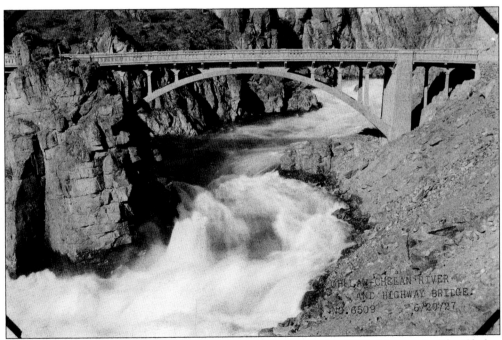

The Chelan River and the old highway bridge are shown in this 1927 photograph. The Chelan River drops almost 400 feet along its 3-mile length, giving the Columbia River settlement its name—Chelan Falls. Lauchlin MacLean was the promoter who organized a group of investors, including Judge Joseph M. Snow and his wife, Sarah J. Snow. Sarah Snow platted 139 acres as the town site of Chelan Falls in February 1891. The first business was the newspaper, the *Chelan Falls Leader*. (Courtesy of the Chelan County PUD.)

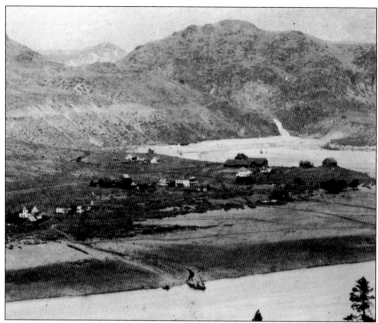

By the end of 1891, Chelan Falls boasted several new businesses in addition to the newspaper, including a sawmill and the Chelan Hotel. A. LaChapelle and his partner ran a steam ferry across the river. The schoolhouse was completed in the fall of 1892. The falls are visible on the right in this 1917 view of the Chelan Falls community from across the Columbia River.

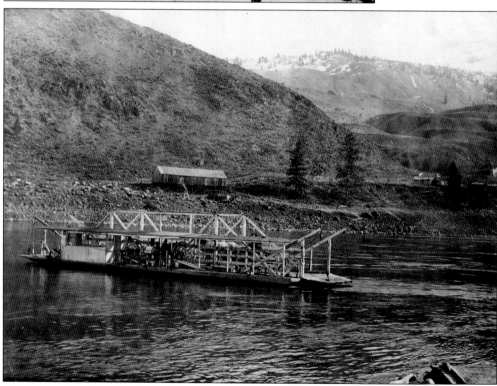

The original Chelan Falls Cable Ferry was owned by MacLean and operated by George Bedtelyou. Mark Ayers purchased the ferry and sold it to James Warren, who operated it until 1914. Charles E. Carter then bought the ferry and operated it until the Beebe Bridge was built in 1919. The ferry used a cable that ran across the river and a winch that would tighten the cable in a way that allowed the boat to cross the river powered by the current.

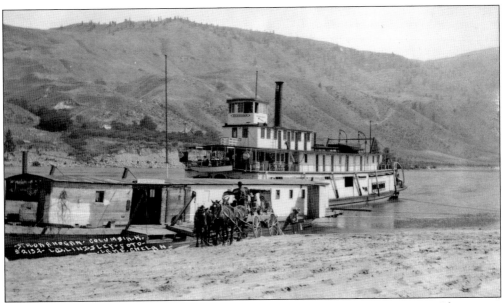

Chelan Falls was a busy terminal for overland and river traffic. Here the steamer *Okanogan* is shown at the docks on March 19, 1914.

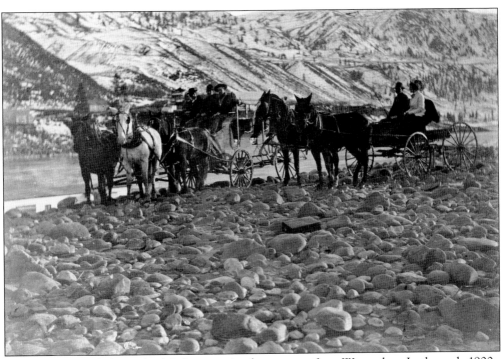

A stagecoach, with driver Art Mathers, awaits the steamers from Wenatchee. In the early 1900s, traveling from Chelan involved a ride on a four-horse stage to Chelan Falls—over a "steep and crooked" road—and a steamboat ride from there to Wenatchee. From there, it was possible to travel on the Great Northern Railway to Seattle.

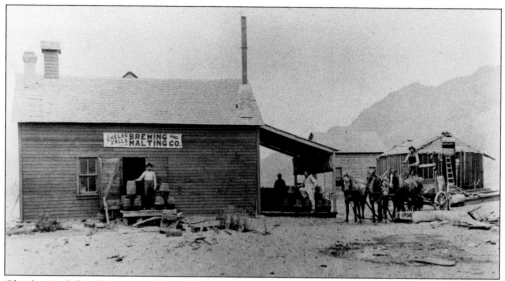

Charles A. Schindler arrived from Minnesota and purchased property in Chelan Falls adjacent to the flour mill. He brought the machinery and fixtures for the brewery from the old Waterville Brewery. By late 1902, business was booming. An advertisement appearing in the newspapers offered "special rates to boats." The brewery operated until 1914.

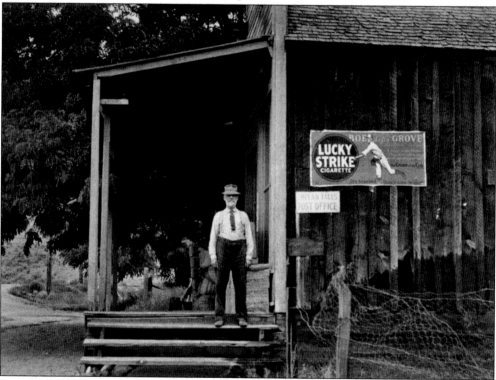

The Chelan Falls Post Office was established in 1891 with DeWitt C. Britt, the editor of the *Chelan Falls Leader*, serving as postmaster. When Britt relocated the newspaper to Chelan in 1892, Judge Joseph M. Snow succeeded him as the Chelan Falls postmaster. Wilbur F. Cobb (shown in this photograph) served as postmaster from 1895 to 1929.

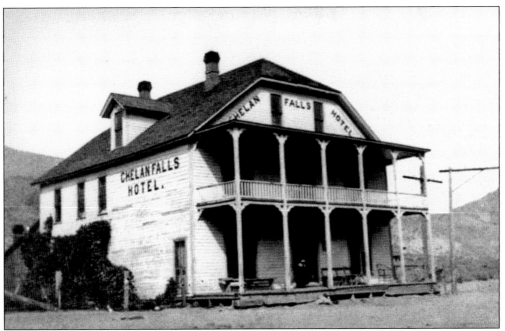

Lauchlin MacLean opened the Hotel Chelan, later known as the Chelan Falls Hotel, in December 1891. It was the only commercial building to escape the flood of June 1894.

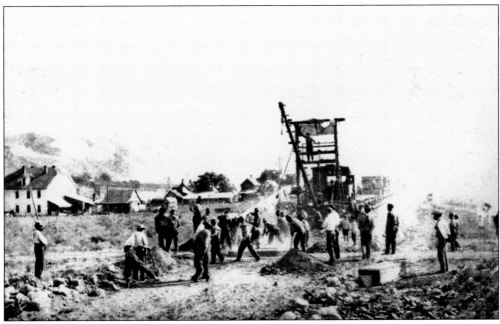

The Great Northern Railway began construction of a railroad line through the middle of the Chelan Falls business district in 1912. The track-laying train came through in 1914, and trains started running on July 1, 1914.

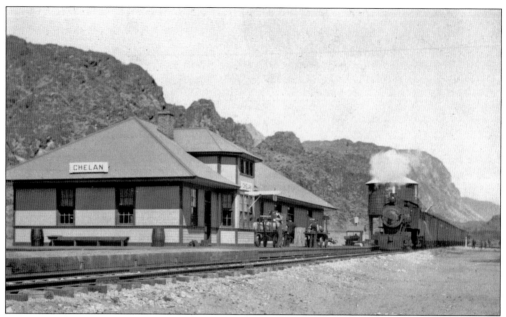

The main Chelan Falls train station was located in the town of Chelan Falls, on the south side of the Chelan River. A second station, known as the Chelan station (shown here), was located north of the river and served Chelan passengers. The train made it possible to make a round-trip to Wenatchee in one day.

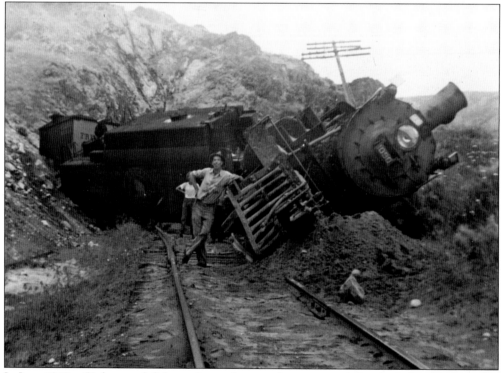

In June 1948, a 50-foot mud slide on the tracks caused a train wreck 2 miles below Chelan Falls. Fortunately, no one was injured in this mishap.

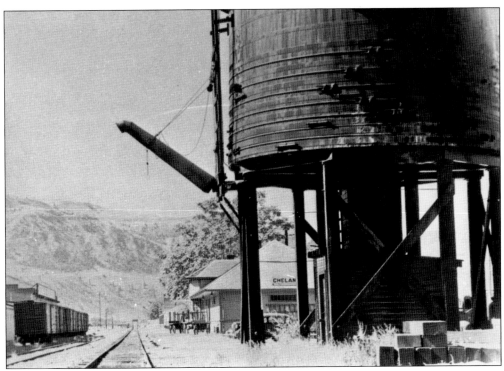

The Chelan rail station is shown behind the water tower.

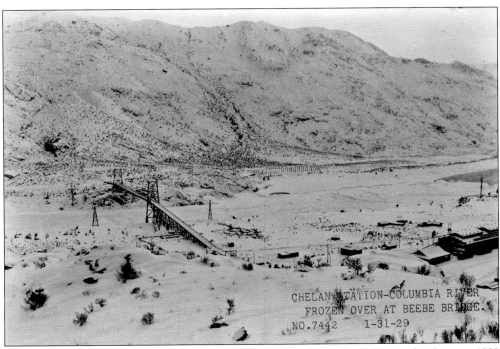

Beebe Bridge—a single-lane wooden structure—was constructed in 1919. In this January 1929 photograph, the Columbia River was frozen over. (Courtesy of the Chelan County PUD.)

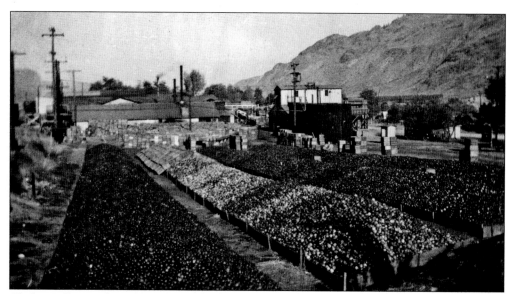

Chelan Falls was the railway shipping point for the agricultural production of the Lake Chelan Valley. Until the railway was extended to Chelan Falls, it served as a hub for steamboat traffic from Wenatchee. With the arrival of the railroad, Chelan Falls became the site of an apple packing facility and a cold-storage warehouse. Here apples are ready for processing.

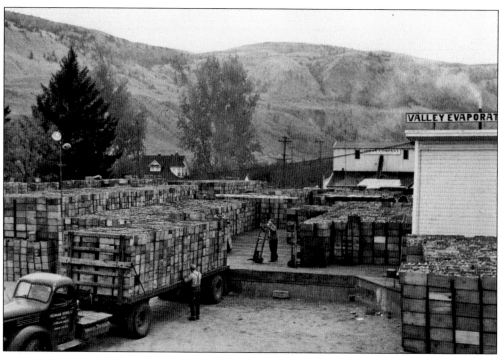

Construction of an apple processing plant in Chelan Falls began in May 1926. The Valley Evaporating Company processed "culls"—apples that were not of sufficient quality to ship to market. Before the processing plant was in operation, the culls were piled up and burned.

Four

LAKE PARK
(LAKESIDE)

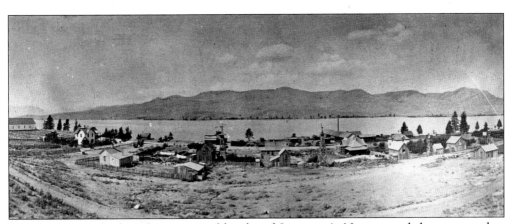

In 1888, Capt. Charles Johnson visited his friend Ignatius A. Navarre and then returned to Nebraska to convince his wife and several family friends to move to the Lake Chelan Valley. In addition to Johnson's family, the families of Ben F. Smith, Tunis Hardenburgh, William Morley, and Ed Emerson made the move. The town site of Lake Park, on the south shore of the lake, was platted June 1891 from parts of the homesteads of Johnson and Hardenburgh. Lake Park had the advantage of deepwater moorage, sufficient to accommodate the steamers that carried supplies and people the length of the lake. The Kingman-Sullins sawmill (shown here) was operating at Lake Park in 1900.

Brothers Alvin (shown here) and Charles Woodin, teenagers at the time, came to the valley in 1887. Their father, Lewis, operated a lumber mill in St. Paul, Minnesota, with a partner, A. F. Nichols. The young men encouraged their father to join them. Lewis immediately saw that the area needed a sawmill. He arranged to close the Minnesota business and ship the equipment to Lake Park. The mill was in operation in October 1888.

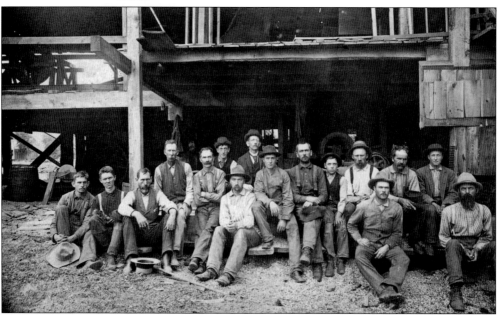

Woodin and Nichols operated the Lake Chelan Lumber Company as well as a small hotel and general store in Lake Park. Workers at the lumber company in 1891 included, from left to right, A. L. Woodin, G. C. Wason, C. Robinson, S. Boyd, D. J. Switzer, C. D. Woodin, C. L. Foster, L. H. Woodin, L. Pershall, E. Merritt, J. Bradley, R. Larson, J. F. Samson, T. A. Wright, T. Pattison, and W. S. McPherron. The sawmill was also known as the Woodin-Nichols Mill.

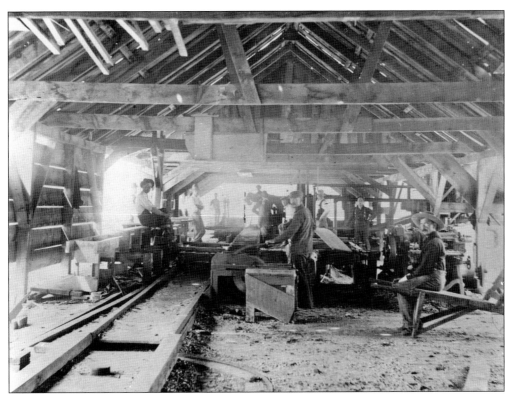

In 1894, H. R. Kingman arrived at Lake Park and started another mill with A. L. Sullins as his partner. This is an interior shot of the Kingman-Sullins Mill.

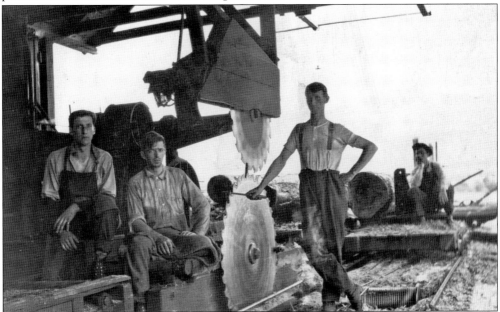

Sawmill workers stand by their equipment in this 1915 photograph that shows the interior of an area sawmill. A worker in the background sits on the carriage that brings the large logs through the saw blade.

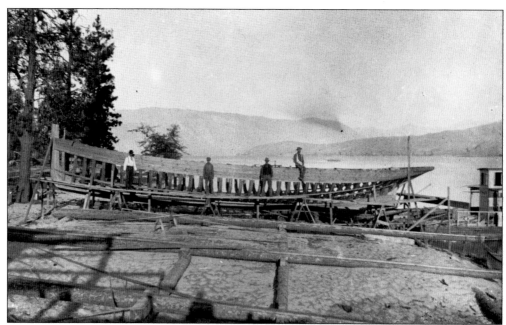

In 1897, Herbert Kingman, owner of the Kingman-Sullins mill, began building the *Swan*, using parts from an early steamer, the *Belle of Chelan*, which was removed from service in 1897. The Cottrell Boatyard in Lakeside completed the work, and on March 14, 1898, the steamer began running mail up-lake and towing logs down-lake to the mill. In 1902, the *Swan*, then owned by W. D. Richards, towed a raft of 600,000 feet of logs down the lake to his mill in Lakeside. Harry Hunt is second from the right. Herbert Kingman is wearing a white shirt.

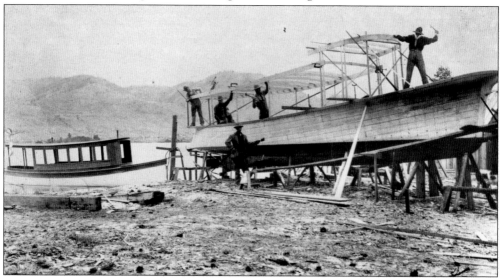

In 1910, the Lake Chelan Boat Company, then owned by George E. Cottrell and the Tuttle family (Bailey J. or "B. J." and his sons Chester and Thomas), built two new boats. The *Rena* was a 30-foot gas-powered boat. The *Comet* was built to handle the company's mail contract, the first gas-powered boat to do so. The *Comet* could travel to Stehekin at the head of the lake in under six hours, making 20 stops along the way. Typically the crew would return the following day after eating their evening meal at the Field Hotel and spending the night on board.

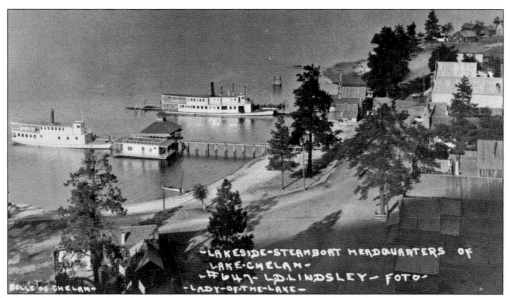

The Lake Chelan Steamboat and Transportation Company was formed in 1905 by Amos Edmunds (the first mayor of Chelan) and August H. Bergman from Minnesota. On July 12, 1905, the Women's Christian Temperance Union hosted the christening of the new *Belle of Chelan* at the Chelan dock, breaking a bottle of water from the Stehekin River's Rainbow Falls on the boat's anchor. Docking in Chelan proved impossible at times as a result of the lack of sufficient water depth, and Bergman gave up trying to make a profit with the boat. E. E. Shotwell acquired control of the *Belle of Chelan* in 1907.

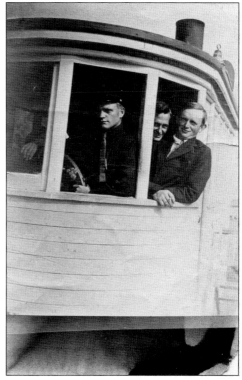

In 1906, the Tourist Company held the mail contract for Lake Chelan. Amos Edmunds and a group of Chelan businessmen financed the construction of the *Tourist*, 64 feet long and 11.5 feet wide with 4-foot draft. A crew of three was typical. Early captains included Roy Smith, Roy Barton, Robert Little, Willard Van Meter, and Ed Merritt. Crew members (engineers and pursers) included E. L. Ward, S. M. Campbell, Jack C. Enlow, Cliff Hendricks, Ted Pasley, and Lou Ward. Robert Little was the captain in 1912, when this photograph was taken.

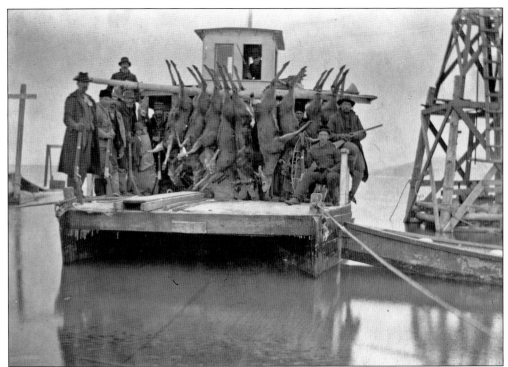

Joe Darnell, owner of the Lake View House Hotel, built a catamaran with a paddle wheel, the *Dragon*, in 1893. In 1897, the *Dragon* was sold to A. J. Dexter, and the boat was renamed the *Dexter*. The *Dexter* served many functions, including being the base for a pile-driving operation and carrying hunting parties. The *Dexter* sank in 1899 after delivering a load of furniture to Clara Little at Granite Falls. After a new caulk job, the *Dexter* returned to service until 1904, when it sank in shallow water off the south shore about 19 miles up-lake.

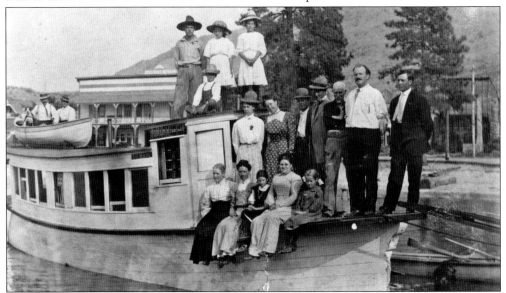

The *Comet*, like most of the Lake Chelan steamers, served general tourists as well as hunting parties.

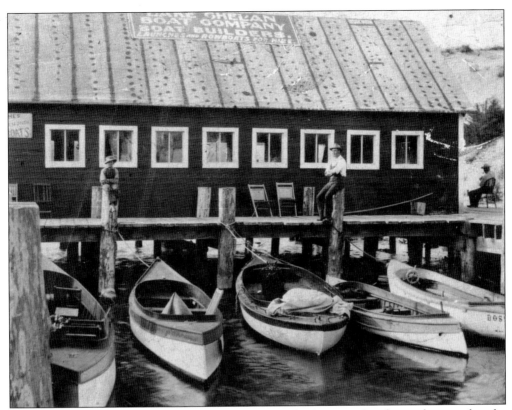

Not all lake traffic was by steamer. Here a row of smaller boats are lined up to be rented at the Lake Chelan Boat Company dock.

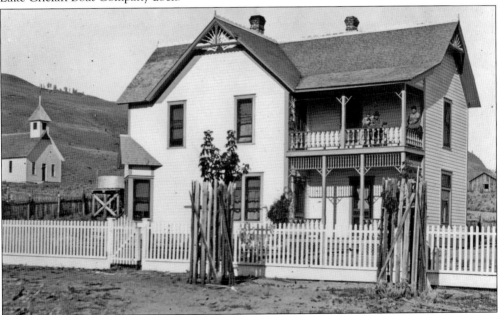

The H. R. Kingman house, originally built in Lakeside, was moved in 1897. Shown on the balcony are Hank, Melissa, and Lawrence Kingman.

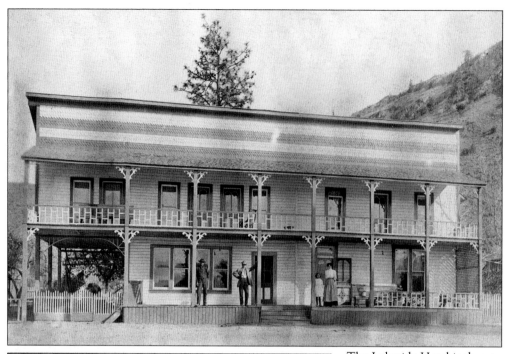

The Lakeside Hotel is shown here when it was owned by Otis Darnell. Included in the photograph are B. G Tuttle, Tom Tuttle, and Nina Tuttle.

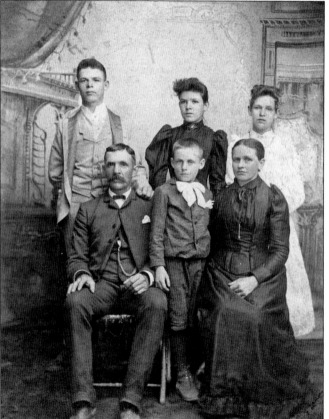

Joseph Darnell arrived in Lake Park from Ohio in 1889 and worked at the sawmill early on. He eventually became manager and then owner of the Woodin Hotel, which later became the Lakeside House. Here Joseph and Nancy are shown with their children, Edward (center, first row) and, from left to right, (second row) Otis, Ella, and Eva.

The Lakeside docks featured an ice cream parlor, shown here at high water.

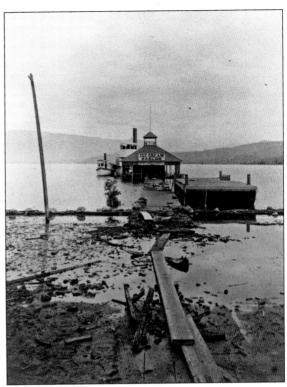

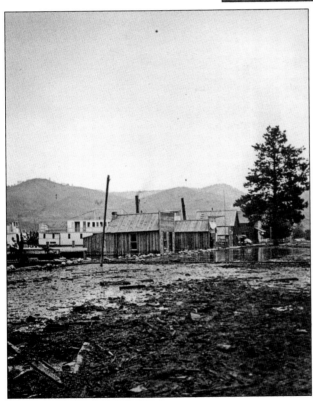

The Lake Park business district flooded if the lake level rose.

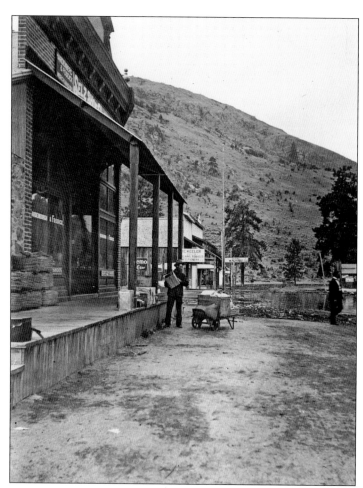

Lakeside was occasionally plagued by high water levels on the lake. This photograph of the Hardenburgh and Fosdick store was taken in 1894, when snowmelt overwhelmed the entire valley and also destroyed much of the business section of the town of Chelan Falls.

A group of recreational boaters is shown here at the Lakeside dock in this photograph from 1905 or earlier. The *Swan* and the *Stehekin* are docked in the background.

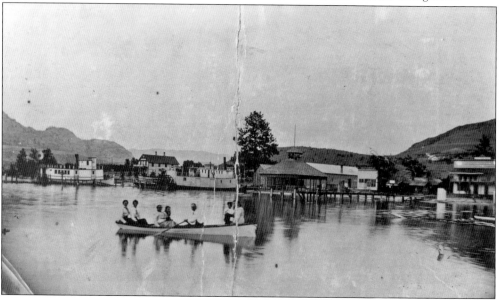

Five

CHELAN

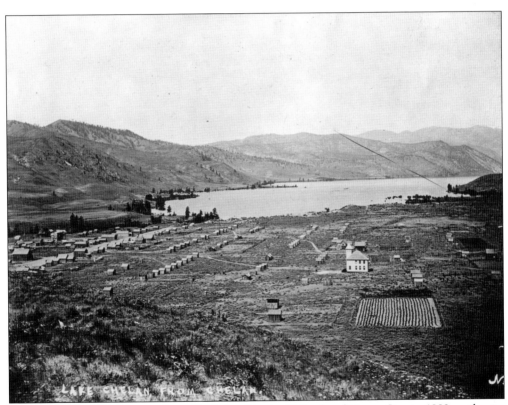

The town site of Chelan was platted by Judge Charles Ballard and Henry Carr in 1889 on the site of Camp Chelan. It was a requirement that buildings be placed on the lots before a deed could be issued. Temporary "houses"—usually 10 by 12 feet in size and not intended for inhabitancy—quickly went up on roughly 300 of the 1,000 lots. There were legal problems with the platting process, which were finally cleared up by an act of Congress. On May 4, 1892, a patent for the town site was issued.

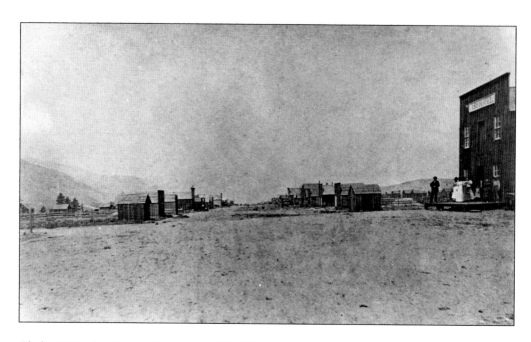

Chelan's Woodin Avenue is shown in 1890 (above). Streets were wide enough for a wagon to turn around. Teams of horses were used to make street improvements. Many of the streets were named after early settlers in the area, including Woodin, Navarre, Sanders, Trow, Robinson, Emerson, Wapato, and Johnson.

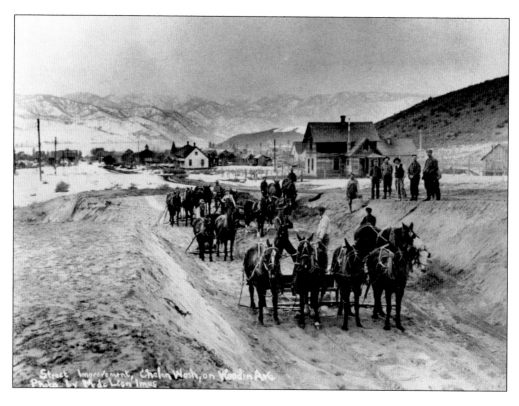

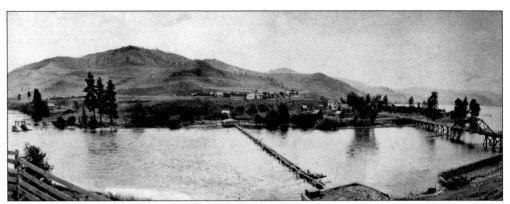

The Woodin-Nichols Sawmill provided lumber for the first bridge over the Chelan River, built in 1889. In 1894, high water caused the north portion of the bridge to collapse, despite the efforts of townspeople to save it. The repair of the bridge resulted in a large hump in the middle of the bridge. Travelers were advised of a "$5 fine for crossing the bridge faster than a walk." A steel structure replaced the wooden bridge in 1912 or 1913. Chelan Butte appears in the background in this photograph.

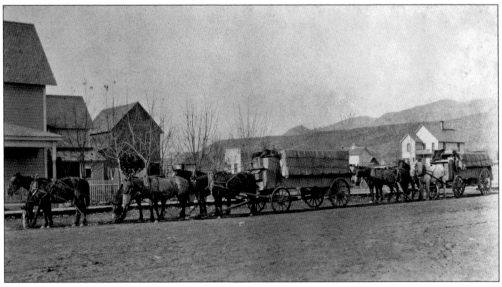

Wagon teams such as these were a common sight in early Chelan.

While apples dominated orchard production in the early years of the valley, grapes and walnuts were also grown. Young Elmer Louis Shepard is shown here in 1902 with some grapes from his family's orchard.

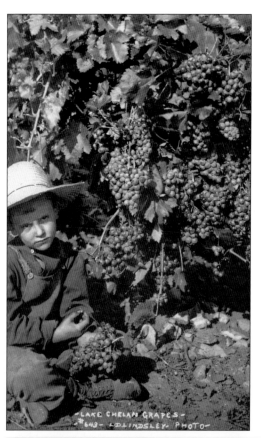

Early in the 1890s, Italians Louis Conti, L. Muoli, and Antonio Pistono formed Conti and Company, intending to produce wine commercially. Production focused on the road to Union Valley, north of Chelan. John Faletto purchased the Conti and Muoli land and continued to grow grapes for personal use. Antonio Pistono remained in the area, proving his homestead in 1896.

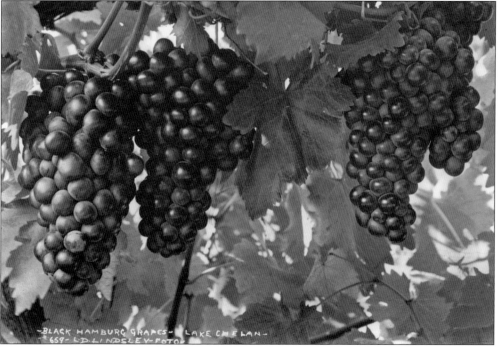

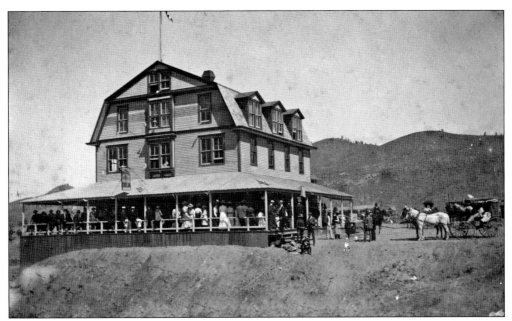

Hotel Chelan held its grand opening in June 1901. Judge Clinton C. Campbell had visited the area in 1889 and purchased several town lots in Chelan. When he returned the next year, A. F. Cox, an architect and builder, accompanied him. Cox designed and built the Campbell home, which was completed in 1890, and the Hotel Chelan, which opened on June 13, 1901. Campbell's goal was "to erect a hostelry that would be a credit to the community."

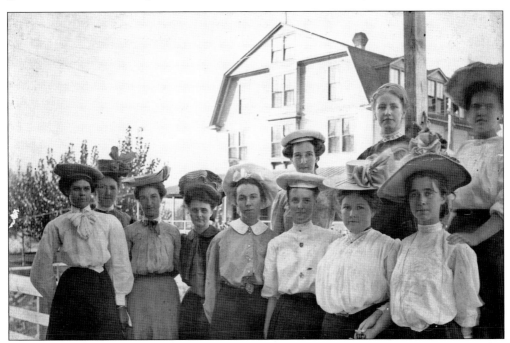

Gathering in front of Campbell's Hotel (formerly the Hotel Chelan) are, from left to right, Mary Budd, Pearl Miller, Edna LaChapelle, Florence Bergman, Ida Jacobs, Bernice Smith, Edith LaChapelle, Ada Riley, Amy Ridenour, Ada Stillwell, and Mabel McPherron.

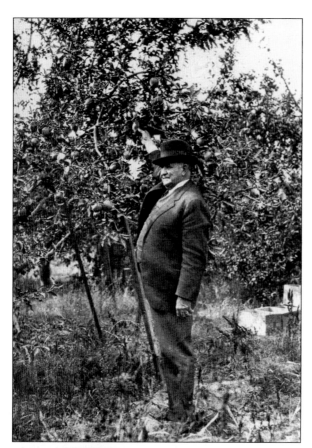

Hon. Clinton C. Campbell had been a magistrate in Sioux City, Iowa. After the town voted itself dry, C. C. was placed in the unenviable position of upholding this unpopular mandate. He decided to head west for new opportunities with less occupational stress. Here he is shown in one of the several orchards he planted in the Chelan area. (Courtesy of Clint Campbell.)

Using wheelbarrows and scoop shovels, Arthur Campbell, the son of C. C. Campbell, excavated the lower level (shown here) of the original Campbell's building in 1916, when a new road providing improved access to the bridge was completed. (Courtesy of Clint Campbell.)

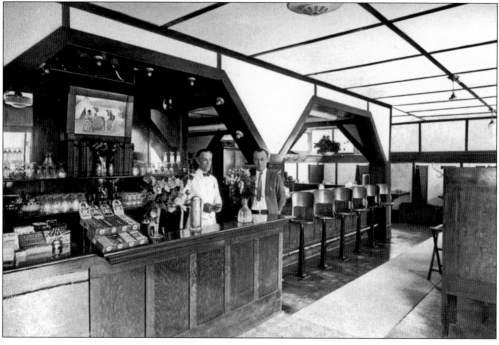

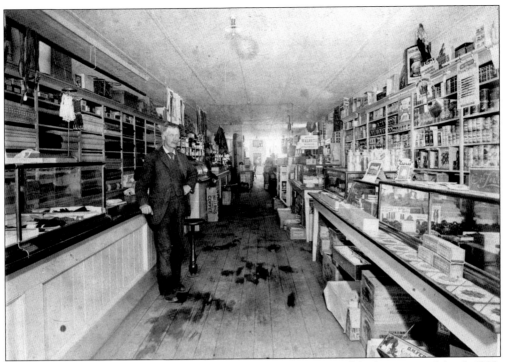

Chelan's first general store, the Whaley General Store, was opened for business on May 6, 1890, with C. E. Whaley (shown here) as proprietor. The Whaley family came from Minnesota.

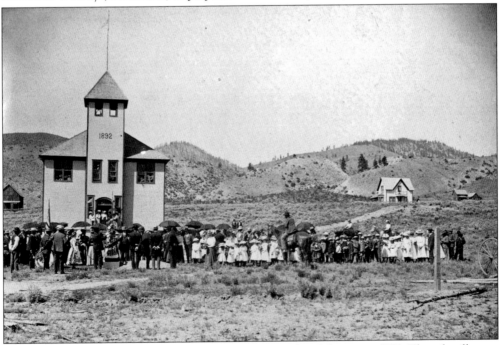

The first school classes held in Chelan were taught by Clara Johnson in 1889. The schoolhouse, a wood structure with one large room, is shown here in a May 30, 1901, photograph. In addition to classes, the building was used for church services, socials, entertainment, and dancing.

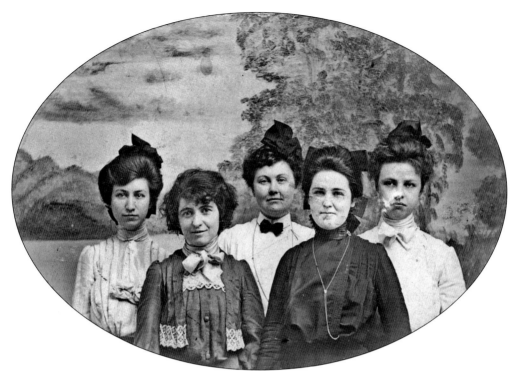

Early Chelan schoolteachers are shown here from left to right: Anna Trisch, Lydia Diehl Switzer, Mary Isenhart, unidentified, and Rose Long Mundt.

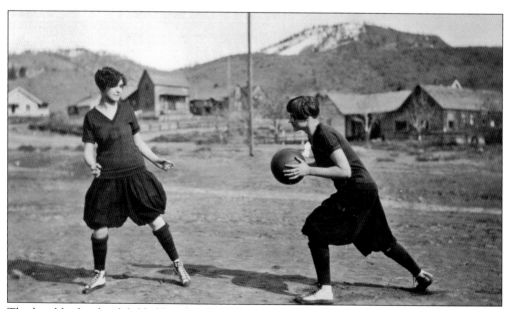

The local high school fielded boys' and girls' teams in several sports. Here two members of the girls' team practice their basketball skills.

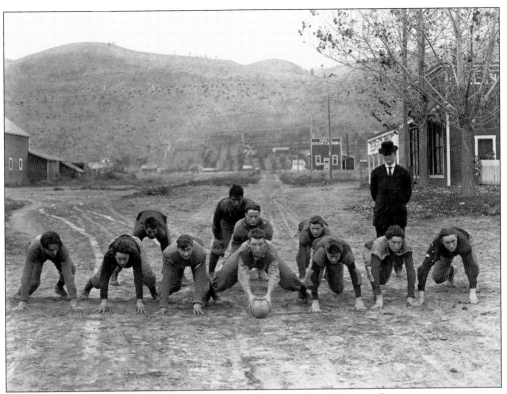

The 1914 Chelan High School football team is shown in this photograph.

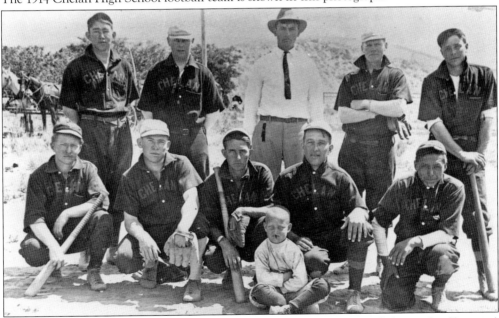

The 1910 Chelan High School baseball team members included, from left to right, (first row) "Doc" Frances Harvey, Bob Brumbley, Roy Duncan, Jake Richardson, Louie Wapato, and Kenny Richardson (mascot); (second row) Vern Richardson, Roy Sines, Harley Farley, Grant Sines, and Claude Wild.

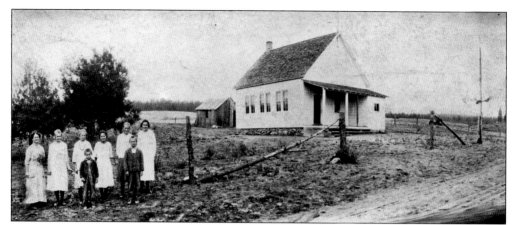

An early Union Valley School photograph shows, from left to right, the teacher, Mrs. Oleson;
Anna Handley; Letha Harris; Edith Handley; Mabel Harris; Catherine Handley; Casey Sawyer;
and Donald Sawyer.

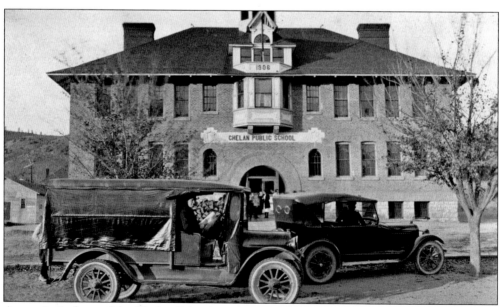

A van sits in front of the Chelan School waiting to pick up schoolchildren. This second school
in Chelan was built in 1906, constructed by H. E. Dunham for $12,000.

52

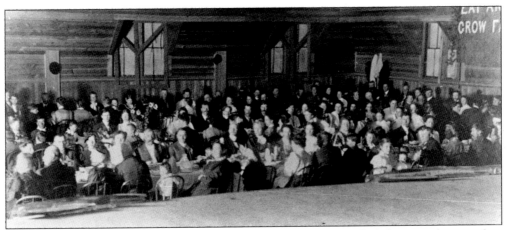

The Old Settlers' Picnic was held in the old auditorium in 1908. Included among the attendees were Judge and Mrs. C. C. Campbell, Dr. and Mrs. Jacobs with their daughter Ida, Otto Hoag, Jennie and Anna Larson, Mr. and Mrs. Spencer Boyd, Mr. and Mrs. W. S. McPherron, Carrie Campbell, Rose Jacobs, and Mary Boyd.

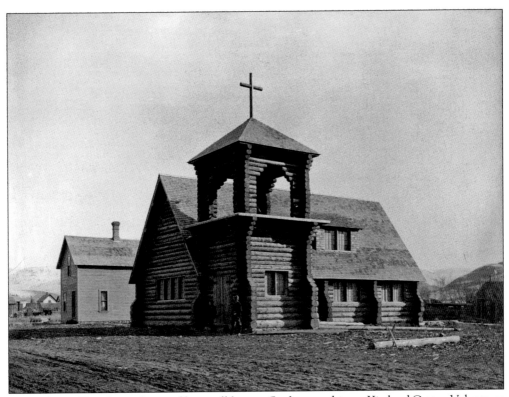

St. Andrew's Church was designed by a well-known Spokane architect, Kirtland Cutter. Volunteers started logging timber for the church in 1896. The church was completed in 1897.

53

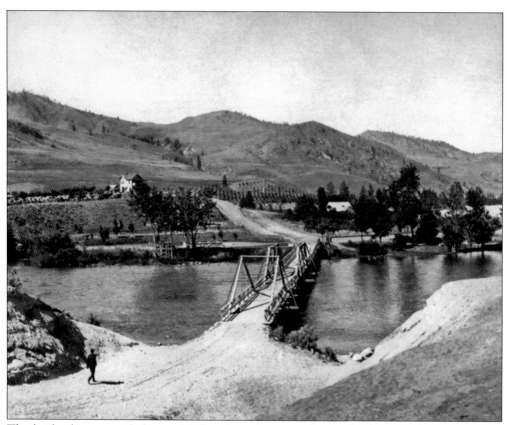

The bridge between Chelan and Lakeside is shown in this early photograph. (Courtesy of Clint Campbell.)

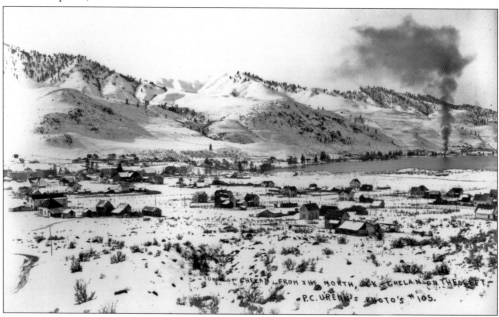

Chelan and Lakeside are seen from the north in this photograph taken February 2, 1910.

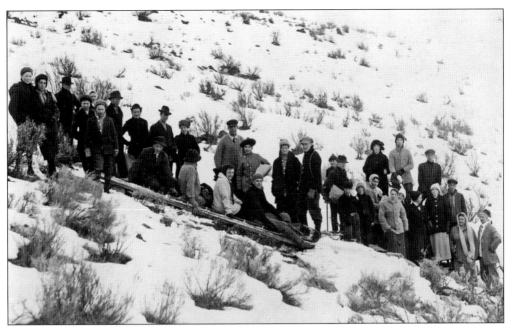

In winter, tobogganing on Long Jim Hill was popular, as was ice-skating on Spader's Bay, on the north shore of the lake by Chelan.

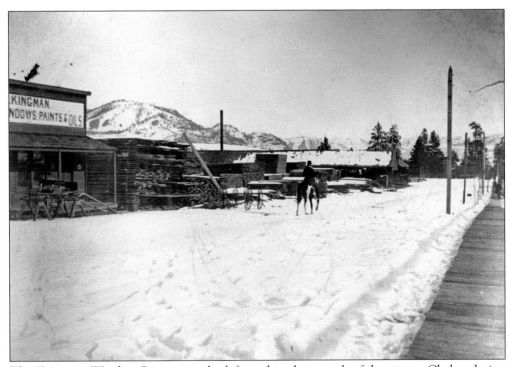

The Kingman Window Store is on the left in this photograph of downtown Chelan during the winter.

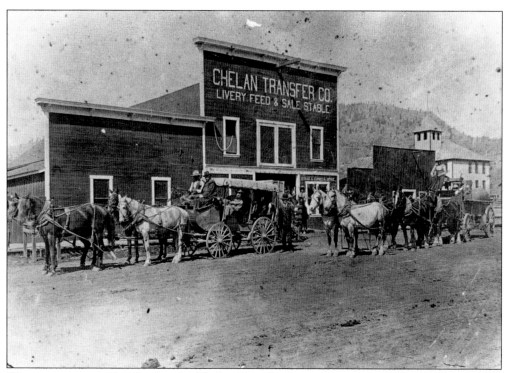

Wagon teams await their load at the Chelan Transfer Company in about 1909. The livery stable provided rental riding and driving horses, and boarding of horses was also provided.

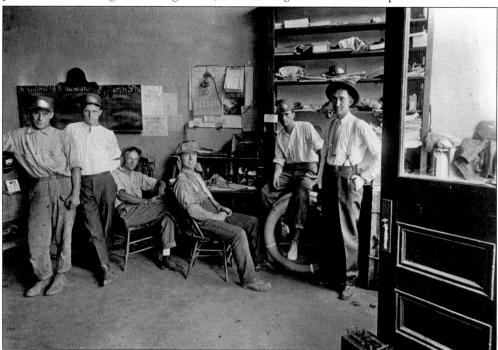

Shown in the office of the Chelan Transfer Company in 1919 are, from left to right, Harlin Livingston, Burel O'Neal, Pete Benson, Bill Spring, Gene Mathers, and Ray Green.

A bicyclist poses in front of the Chelan Transfer Company.

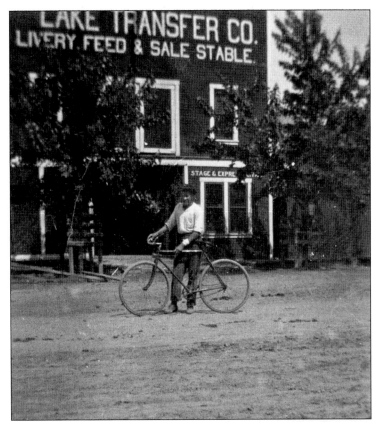

The Chelan-Brewster mail carrier, Frank M. C. Wammer, is shown in this photograph taken in 1902 or 1903.

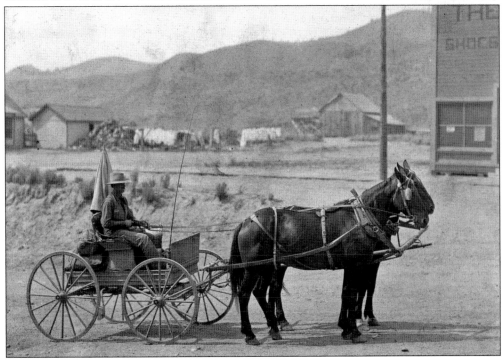

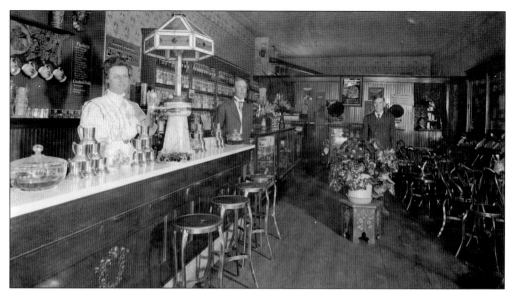

John Mundt arrived in Chelan in 1906 and opened his Red Cross Pharmacy, Mundt's Drug Store, on June 2 of that year. In 1919, he expanded his business to add a soda fountain. Mundt was a pharmacist in Chelan for 32 years.

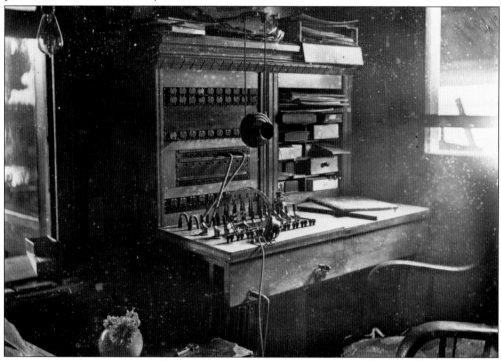

The Pacific States Telephone Company brought telephone service to Chelan in 1902. The first switchboard was installed in the back of Murdock's Chelan Hardware and Furniture Store. In 1908, the switchboard was moved to Mundt's Drug Store, shown here. Mundt purchased the system in 1911, and the name was changed to the Chelan Valley Telephone and Telegraph Company. Smaller communities around the lake had their own private telephone systems. Members purchased their own telephones, wire, and insulators and installed the systems themselves.

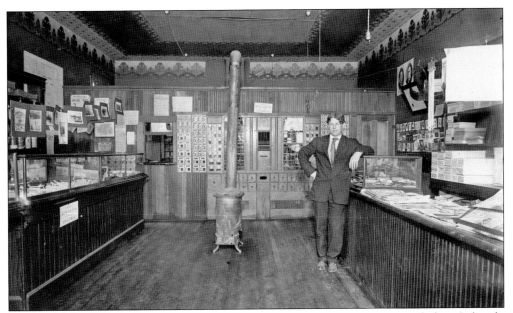

Rev. Henry Gurr was an Episcopal priest, and his family lived in many places, including Colorado and Alaska, before he was assigned to St. Andrew's Episcopal Church in Chelan. Shortly after his arrival, he purchased a Chelan jewelry store. His son, William E. Gurr, visited him from Alaska and decided to move to Chelan. He took watch-making classes in Minneapolis and took over the jewelry store when he returned to Chelan. In 1906, the Chelan Post Office was located in Gurr's Jewelry Store, shown here. Bill Gurr was an avid photographer, and he expanded his business to include photography supplies.

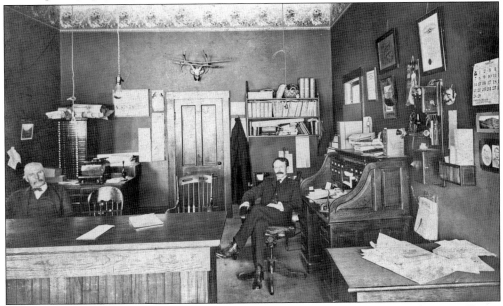

Amos Edmunds, Chelan's first mayor, and Chester Ridout are shown in their real estate office in 1910. Amos Edmunds, who was married to Mary Campbell, the sister of C. C. Campbell, arrived in 1900. He had been a cattle breeder, dairy farmer, and cheese manufacturer. In addition, he had served in the Illinois State Legislature.

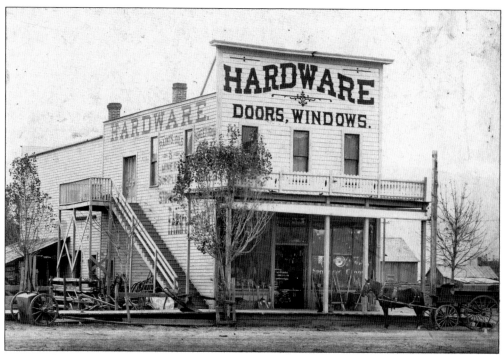

Roy Smith worked for Darius Murdock, proprietor of Murdock's Hardware, and purchased the business when Murdock moved to Waterville.

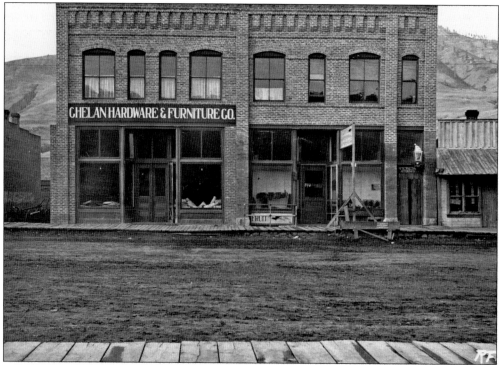

Another business in early Chelan was the Chelan Hardware and Furniture Company, housed in one of the attractive brick buildings of the early days.

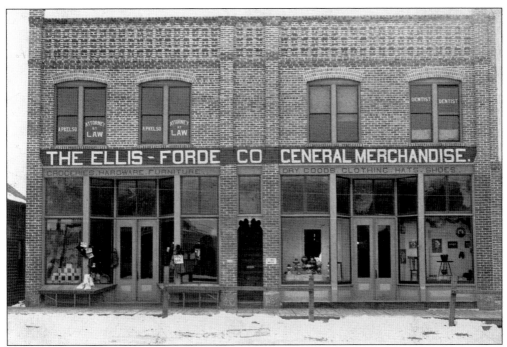

The Ellis-Forde General Merchandise building is shown in 1904. John Isenhart, Ed Gody, and Mrs. Wood are shown inside the store in 1910. The building—built in 1902 by Gene Dunham, owner of a local brickyard—was one of seven stores in the region owned by George E. Ellis Jr. and James E. Forde. On one side of the store were groceries, hardware, and furniture, and on the other were dry goods, clothing, hats, and shoes. A stairway between the stores led to apartment and office space on the upper floor.

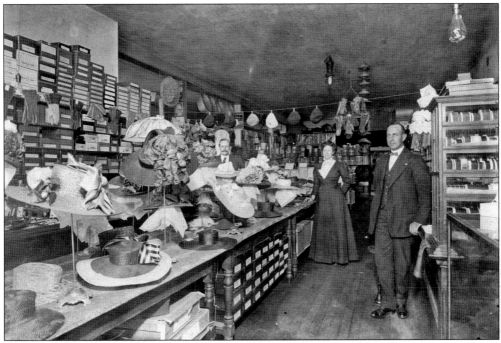

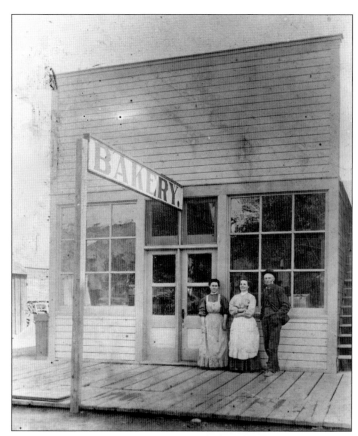

Funk's Bakery opened in about 1907. Shown in front of the store from left to right are Mrs. Henderson, Mrs. Frank Funk, and Frank Funk. Shown below is the interior of the bakery.

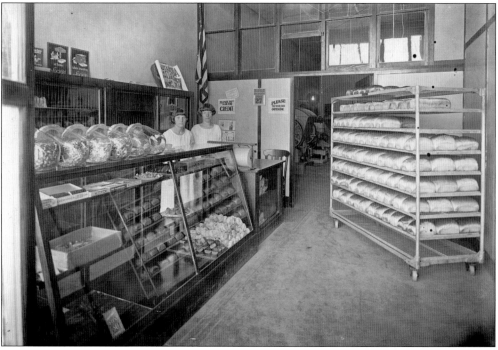

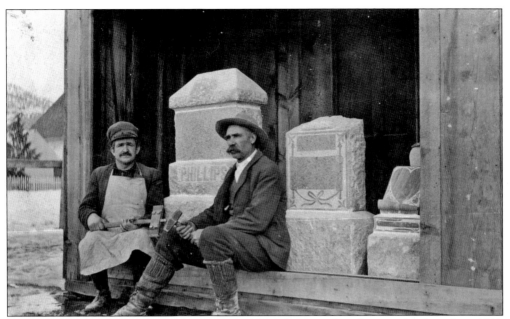

Tombstone carvers Mr. Rucker and John W. Budd are shown in this photograph taken about 1910. The oldest organized cemetery in the Chelan area was the Mount Olivet Cemetery. Members of the Mount Olivet Cemetery Association in 1901 were Clara G. Budd, Carrie E. Campbell, Sadie Berrier, Minnie F. Carlisle, Rosa Whaley, J. W. Budd, Willard H. Roots, C. C. Campbell, C. E. Whaley, William Gibson, and A. H. Murdock.

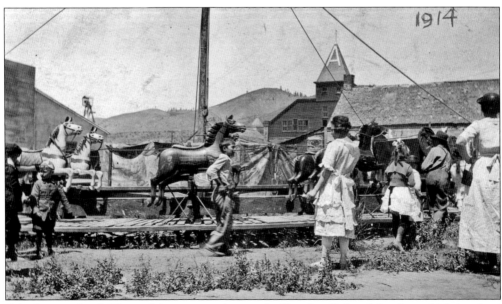

A high point for children of the community was the Fourth of July celebration, which involved several days of special events, including this carnival in 1914.

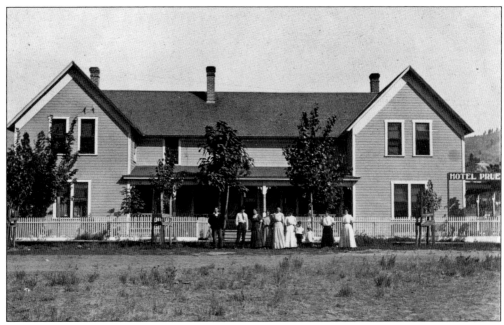

The Hotel Pruett on the corner of Sanders Street and Johnson Avenue is shown here in about 1906.

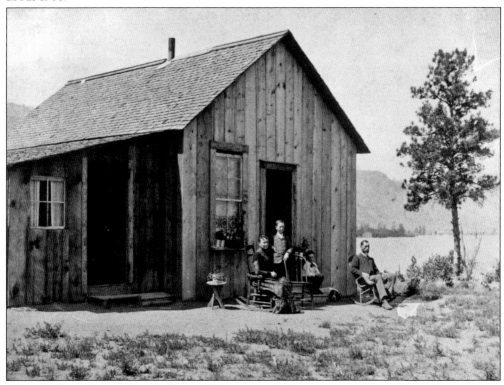

Ellen, William Charlie, Frank C., and Christopher Robinson are shown in front of their home in Chelan. Christopher Robinson worked for Woodin and Nichols mill in Minnesota and was responsible for shipping the equipment for the Woodin-Nichols mill from St. Paul to Chelan.

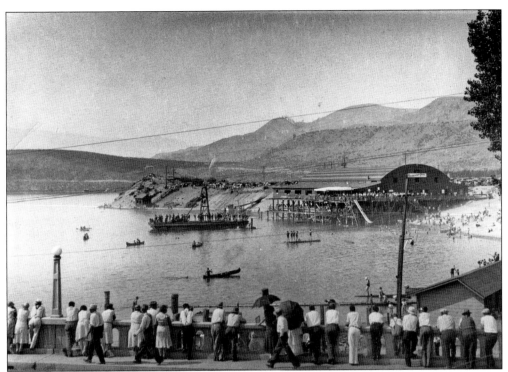

Through most of the 1930s, Chelan's recreation park on the lake provided a popular gathering place. It was destroyed by fire a few years after this photograph was taken.

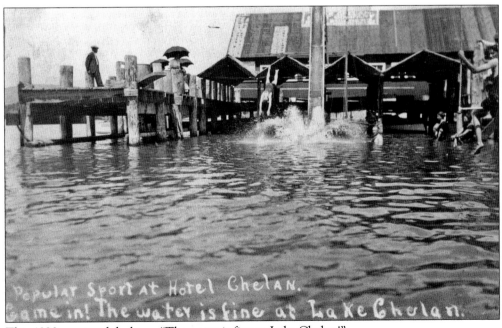

This 1920s postcard declares, "The water is fine at Lake Chelan!"

The road into Chelan from the south traversed Knapp's Hill. Until a tunnel was built, many automobiles would make multiple stops on the way up to allow their cars to cool down. Some cars had to drive backward to allow gas to flow into the motor. The tunnel was built in 1938, allowing traffic to take the easier and more direct route.

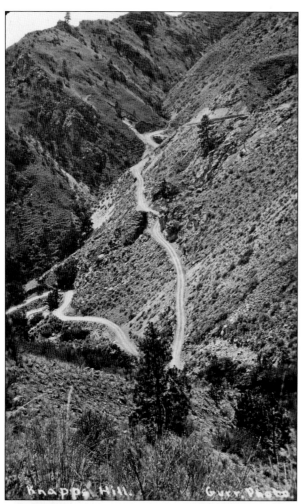

Knapp's Hill.   Gurr Photo

The Lake Transfer Company was the first auto for hire in Chelan. William Spring was the driver.

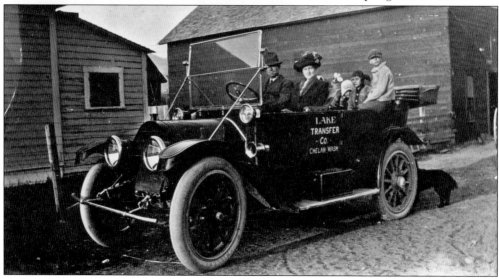

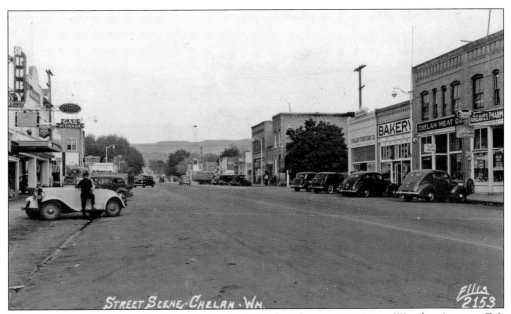

Morrison M. and Herbert R. Kingman built the Ruby Theater in 1914 on Woodin Avenue. F. J. Potter managed the theater and named it for his foster daughter Ruby.

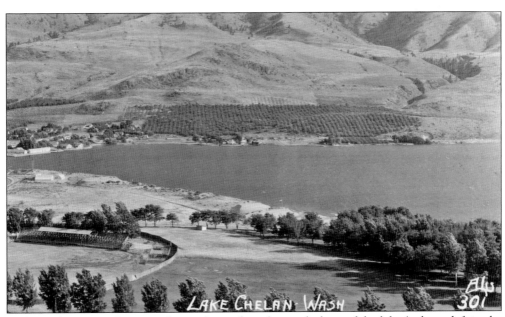

In the early years, rodeo grounds were located on the north shore of the lake (at lower left in the photograph). The Lake Chelan City Park is now located on this site.

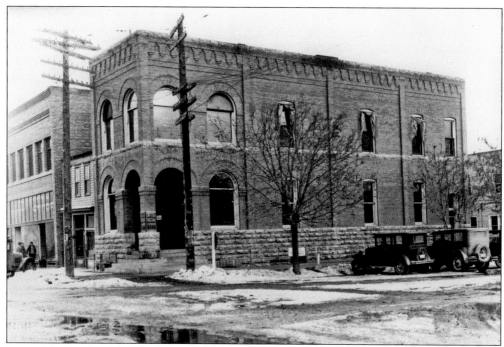

One of the first brick buildings in Chelan was built for the Chelan Bank, which was founded in 1893 by Joshua F. Baker and F. S. Converse. The basement and lower part of the building were made of granite quarried about 3 miles from Chelan. The name of the bank was changed to the Miners and Merchants Bank in 1902. The building is now the headquarters of the Lake Chelan Historical Society.

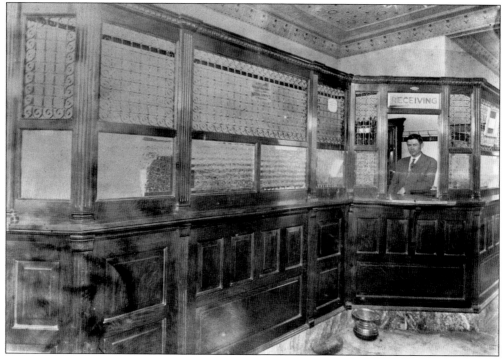

Six

MANSON

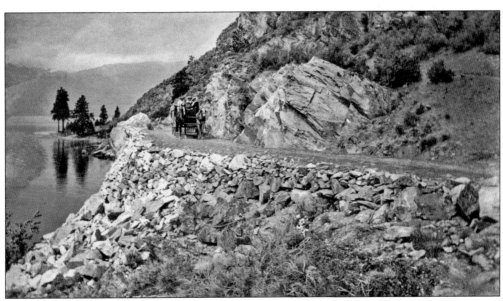

One of the most difficult parts of the land journey between Chelan and the Manson area was over or around a cliff known as Rocky Point. Increased apple production around Manson led to the carving of a one-lane road around the point. Previously, the route went over Rocky Point. Obed Stanford was the foreman for the construction of this road, completed in 1916.

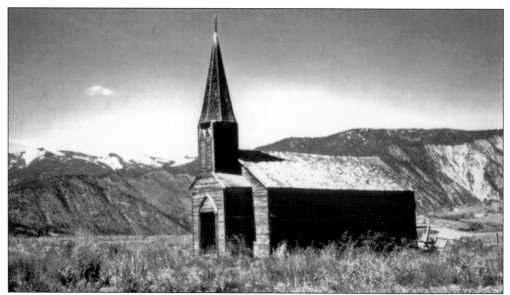

Early on, Wapato John wanted a church built on his land on Mill Bay. At the time, he was a successful farmer and raised cattle. Ben Martin owned a store across the Columbia River in Douglas County but wanted to relocate to the Lake Chelan area. He traded the lumber in his store with Wapato John for eight calves. The Wapato family transported the lumber 30 miles from its original location to the church site. St. John the Baptist Catholic Church was completed in 1888, and Wapato John was authorized by the Catholic Church to conduct services. The church, last used for Peter Wapato's funeral in 1949, was destroyed by fire in 1953.

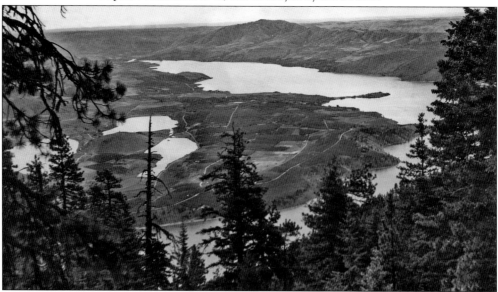

Looking down over the Manson area down-lake, the three lakes above Manson (Wapato Lake, Roses Lake, and Dry Lake) are clearly visible in the foreground. Wapato Point is the narrow peninsula extending into the lake. Manson Bay is just up-lake from Wapato Point, while Mill Bay is just down-lake. After the area was opened to general homesteading in 1886, the first settlers included Ben Martin, who was persuaded by Peter Wapato to make the move from Douglas County, and Martin Venneburg. (Photograph from the Gale Courtney collection; courtesy of Dennis King.)

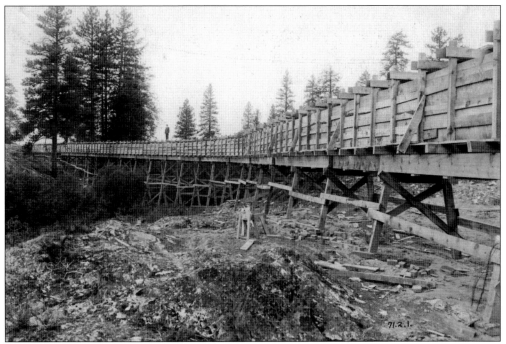

In 1911, A. Bergman supervised the grading of 100 acres for the new town site of Manson. Manson was named for Manson Backus, the father of LeRoy M. Backus, president of the Lake Chelan Land Company. At that time, the company owned 6,500 acres and had plans to irrigate and subdivide it into parcels suitable for agricultural operations. Flume construction for the irrigation works would require vast amounts of lumber. The earliest irrigation efforts involved capturing water from nearby creeks and transporting it to irrigated areas by board flumes such as these.

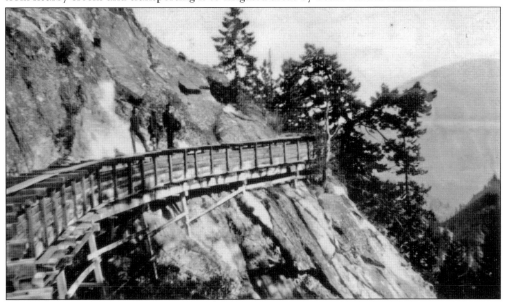

Construction of the flumes in the rugged terrain of the area proved challenging. Trails were built along the flumes so workers could access them for repairs relatively easily. Throughout the 1920s, irrigation flumes were added up-lake, eventually reaching Safety Harbor.

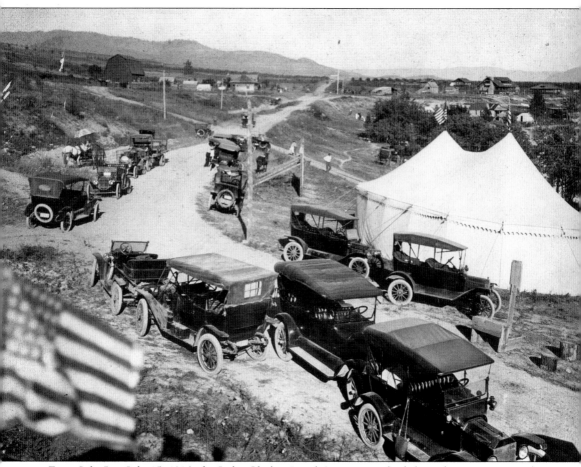

From July 5 to July 15, 1916, the Lake Chelan Land Company, which brought irrigation to the district, auctioned off plots of land. The real estate firm of Furey, East, Pfau, and Gordon, Inc.,

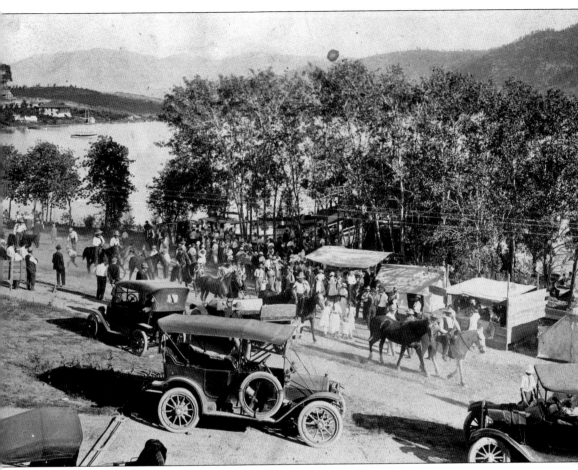

served as brokers for the real estate transactions.

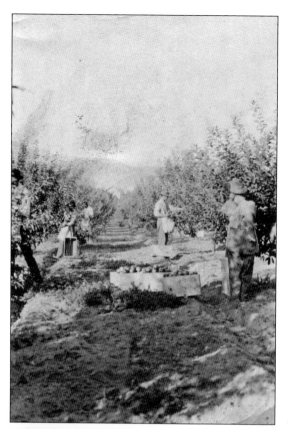

Peter Wapato and Ben Martin had each planted apple orchards before 1890. In the early days, each tree was hand-irrigated with holes dug at the base of the tree and water carried in by hand until ditches or flumes were constructed. School was closed for two weeks in the fall so that older children could help with the harvest. Apples were sometimes trucked to Wenatchee and sometimes to Chelan Falls for shipment by rail. By the 1920s, some orchard owners sorted and packed their own harvest, affixing distinctive labels for their orchard to the side of the packing boxes.

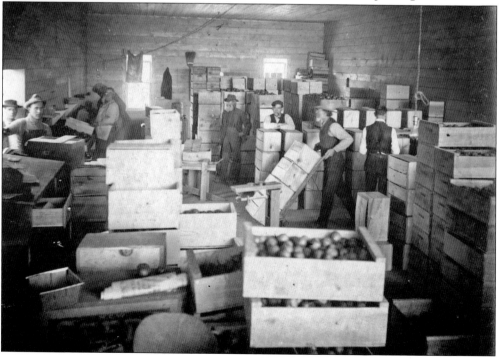

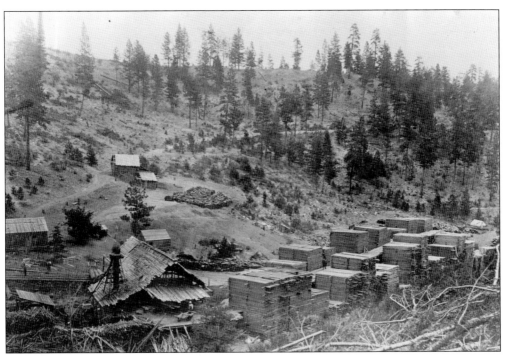

The Coleman and Despain mill at Bear Wallow near Antilon Lake was a major supplier of lumber for the irrigation works around Manson.

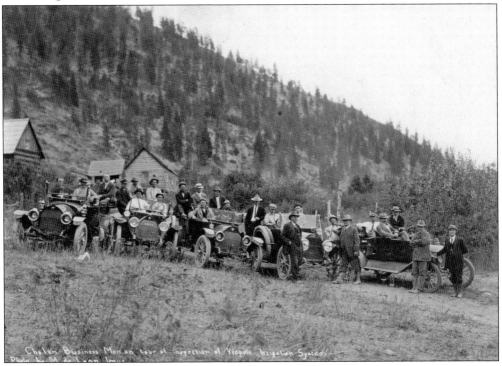

The irrigation project around Manson was developed initially by speculators. Potential investors from Chelan were invited to tour the project.

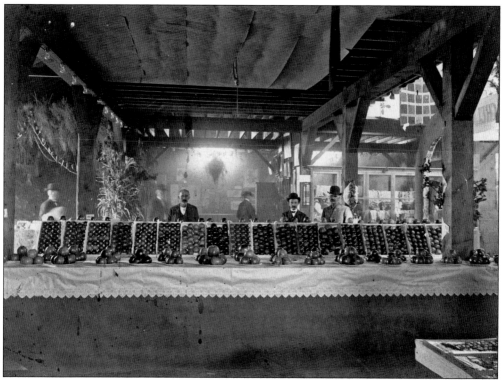

Displays of Lake Chelan fruit and vegetables at expositions all around the United States inspired many families to move to the Lake Chelan Valley.

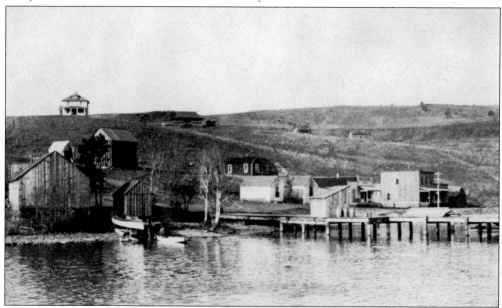

The original town of Manson was built west of the current town and at a lower elevation. When the lake level was raised in 1927, these buildings were either demolished or relocated to higher elevations. Lumber for the Manson Store was brought in by boat since the road around Rocky Point had not been constructed.

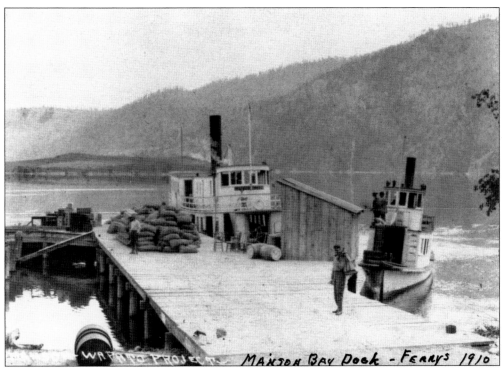

In 1910, a ferry ran between Manson and the First Creek area across the lake. Wapato Point is in the background. (From the Irma Keeney collection; courtesy of Dennis King.)

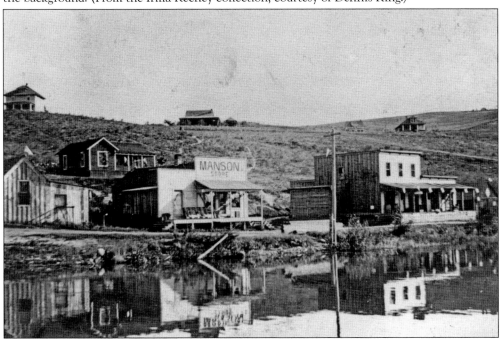

By 1914, Manson had a general store with a post office inside, a barbershop, Blanchard's Eating House, a drugstore, and a land office. The Sherman Bell house is seen on the upper left. (From the Irma Keeney collection; courtesy of Dennis King.)

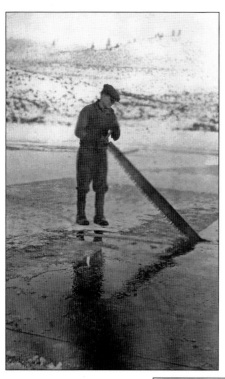

Ice that lasted well into the following summer was cut from the Manson Bay or from the lakes above Manson. Here Tom Kussmaul is cutting ice from Wapato Lake. (Courtesy of Dennis King.)

Art and Billie Legg arrived in Manson at the urging of Billie's uncle, Tom Kussmaul. When she stepped out of her uncle's Model T Ford into 6 inches of dust, she was ready to turn around and go right back to California. Perhaps she had adjusted to the lifestyle by the time winter rolled around. (Courtesy of Dennis King.)

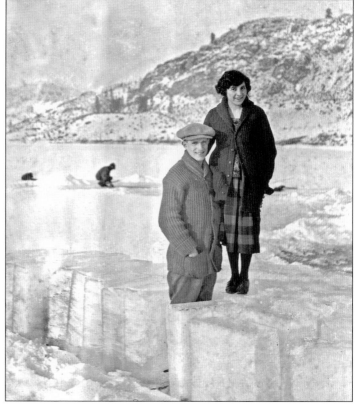

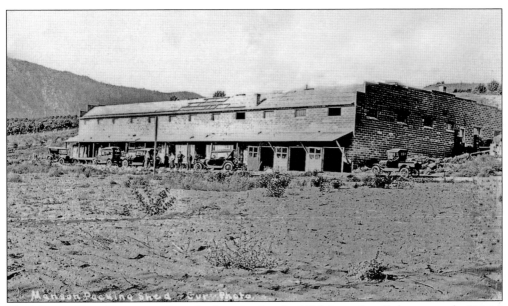

The Manson Fruit Growers packing shed was in place by 1925. It was locally known as the "Unit" packing shed. (From the Terry Urness collection; courtesy of Dennis King.)

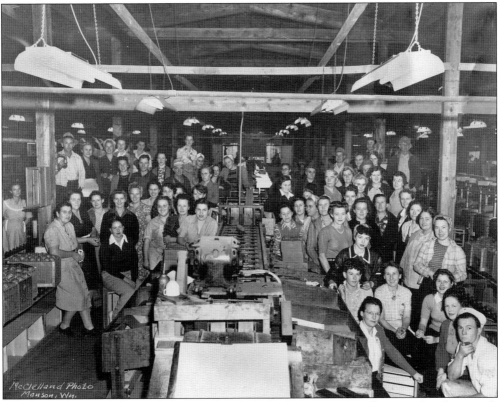

Workers at the Lake Chelan Fruit Growers packing shed in Manson are shown in this photograph taken in the fall of 1946. Apple packing operations continued through 1976 at this location. (From the Dude and Mary Davis collection; courtesy of Dennis King.)

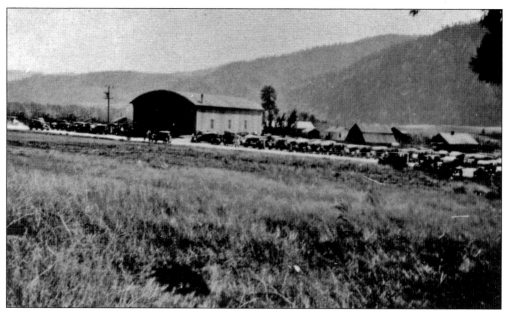

Manson community members raised funds and joined together to build the Manson Community Hall. Henry Barnes designed the building, including the trusses for the curved roof. A. N. Banks was in charge of fund-raising. Construction started in the spring of 1923, and by the early summer of 1924, the building was the focal point for community activities, including dances, plays, banquets, minstrel shows, band practices and concerts, and Apple Blossom Festival programs. High school basketball teams used the facility for games until 1952, when the high school added a gymnasium at the school site. (From the Irma Keeney collection; courtesy of Dennis King.)

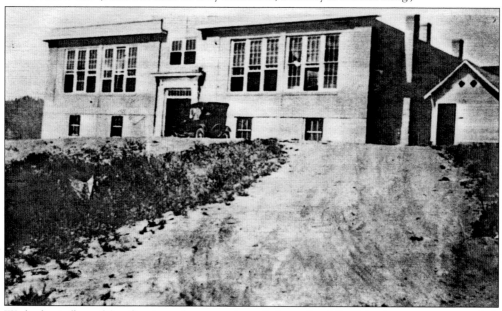

With the influx of families into the area, the existing school facilities became overcrowded. A new schoolhouse was built on the hill above Manson on land donated by the Lake Chelan Land Company. The school is shown here as it was in 1925. (From the Irma Keeney collection; courtesy of Dennis King.)

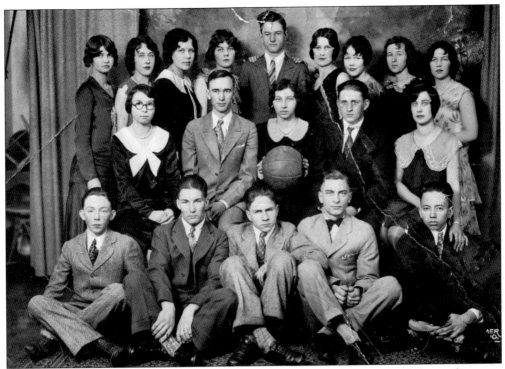

The Manson High School basketball teams shown here (1928, above, and 1930) were fortunate to have practiced and played their games in the Manson Community Hall. Until that facility was available to the community, the teams used the pavilion built out over the water in Manson Bay. Gas lanterns hoisted up into the rafters provided light. Steel rods ran across the building to hold the two sides together. Players shooting from behind the foul line had to arc their shots over these rods. (Above courtesy of Dennis King; below from the Irma Keeney collection, courtesy of Dennis King.)

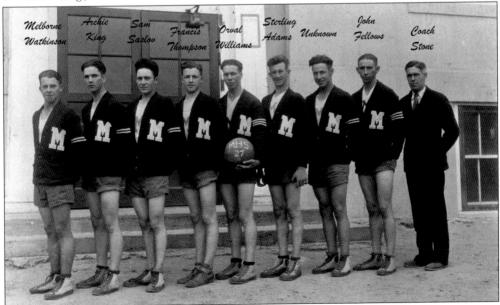

Melborne Watkinson, Archie King, Sam Saslov, Francis Thompson, Orval Williams, Sterling Adams, Unknown, John Fellows, Coach Stone

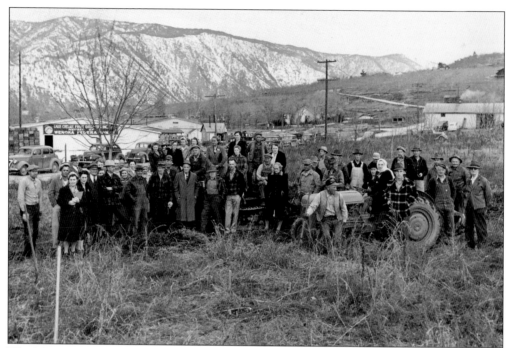

The Manson Grange was organized April 3, 1923, with 48 members. Through the years, the Grange supported many local projects, including sponsorship of the Manson Apple Blossom Festival, the community band, mosquito-control efforts, the regional library, and 4-H clubs. In March 1947, ground was broken for the Manson Grange Hall, which was dedicated on April 3, 1948. (Courtesy of Dennis King.)

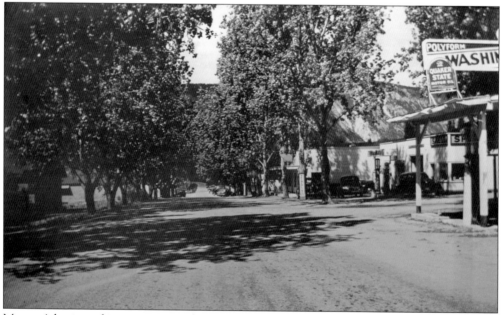

Manson's business district was expanding. By 1925, Manson had two stores, a post office, a garage, and a public library. By 1925, a hardware store, a barber and beauty shop, and a drugstore had been added to the downtown. (Courtesy of Dennis King.)

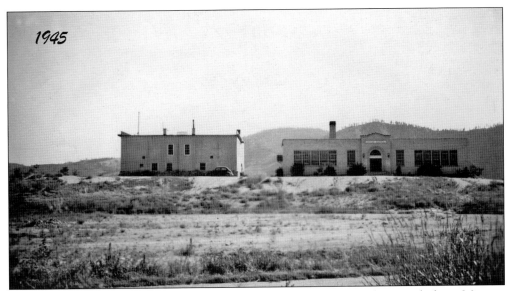

1945

In 1931, bonds were issued for a new grade school building. This 1945 photograph shows Manson High School on the left and Manson Elementary School on the right. (From the Roger Stanford collection; courtesy of Dennis King.)

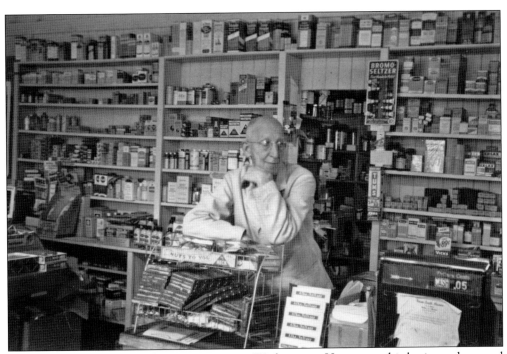

Henry Vercoe had been a druggist in western Washington. He gave up his business there and moved to the drier climate of the Lake Chelan area because of bronchial asthma. He first worked in Lester Morse's orchard. With improving health, he was able to occasionally fill in as a pharmacist at Mundt's Drug and Grocery in Chelan. In 1932, he became the pharmacist at Mundt's pharmacy in Manson and worked there until his retirement. (From the Charlotte Hubbard collection; courtesy of Dennis King.)

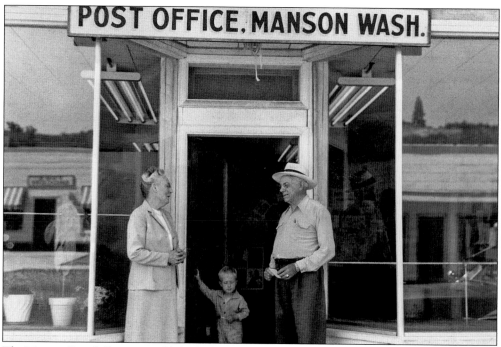

The Manson Post Office was established July 19, 1912, and was housed in Arthur Watkinson's general store. In the early years, the mail was delivered three times per week by steamer. By 1919, the road between Chelan and Manson was good enough to establish a star route with daily delivery. In 1923, Carl Jensen became postmaster and encouraged the local residents to petition for a rural route. The first rural route out of Manson was 26.6 miles in length. Shown here, in a 1951 photograph, are Ester Boaz, the postmaster (left); Dr. Isaac G. Hubbard on the right; and Jon Hubbard standing between them. (From the Charlotte Hubbard collection; courtesy of Dennis King.)

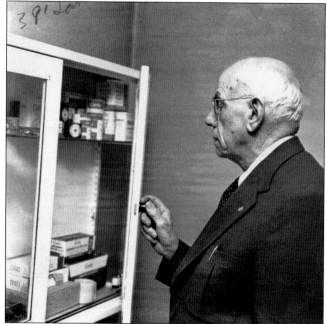

An apple exhibit by the Chelan Land Company at the Illinois State Fair inspired Dr. Isaac G. Hubbard and his brother Edward Hubbard, a dentist, to invest in a 20-acre four-year-old apple orchard. They hired an orchard manager and returned to their practices in Illinois. Except for a summer visit with his family in 1918, Dr. Hubbard did not return to the area until 1928, at which time he expected to sell the orchard and go back to Illinois. Instead, after discovering that the area needed a doctor, he decided to stay, practicing in Manson for another 30 years. (From the Charlotte Hubbard collection; courtesy of Dennis King.)

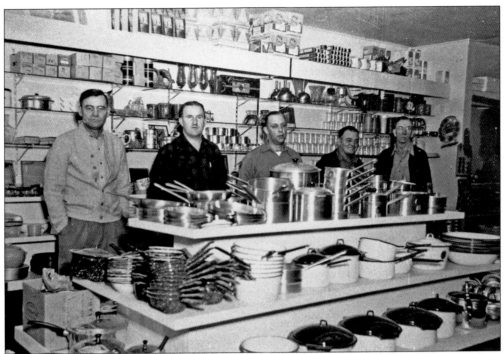

The Manson Supply Company in 1942 was owned by Modest Peters (left). Employees were, from left to right, J. V. DeWalt, Harry Hudson, Paul Brown, and Dick Barrington. (From the Terry Urness collection; courtesy of Dennis King.)

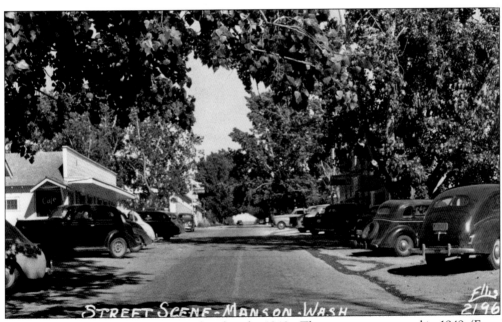

Downtown Manson streets were tree-lined in the 1940s. The trees were removed in 1949. (From the Charlotte Hubbard collection; courtesy of Dennis King.)

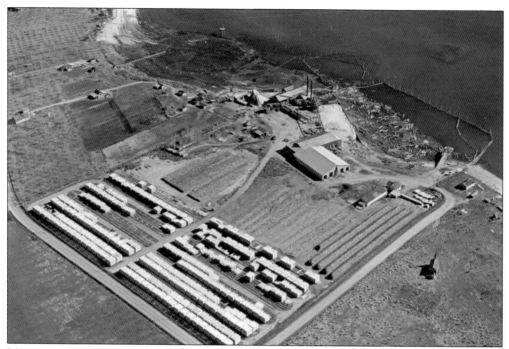

Manson area residents grew accustomed to the sound of the factory whistles of the Chela Box and Manufacturing Company starting in 1931. The company, with a large factory and sawmill on Mill Bay, was one of the area's major employers with two shifts of 80 workers each at its peak. Using logs rafted in from up-lake, the factory produced wooden apple boxes as well as bundles of box pieces—"shook"—for orchardists who elected to assemble their own boxes. Commercial lumber was also produced. Over time, larger bins placed in orchards reduced the demand for the company's small apple boxes and the box factory part of the business closed in 1967. The company continued to mill and sell commercial lumber until January 9, 1969, when a fire destroyed the mill. (Courtesy of Linda Martinson.)

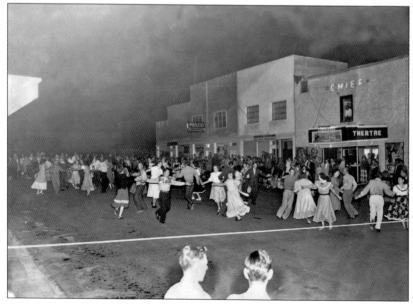

Square dancers took over Wapato Way, Manson's main street, in celebration of the new street in 1945–1946. The Chief Theatre is visible in the background. (From the Sandy and Gary Miller collection; courtesy of Dennis King.)

Seven

DAMS AND HYDROPOWER

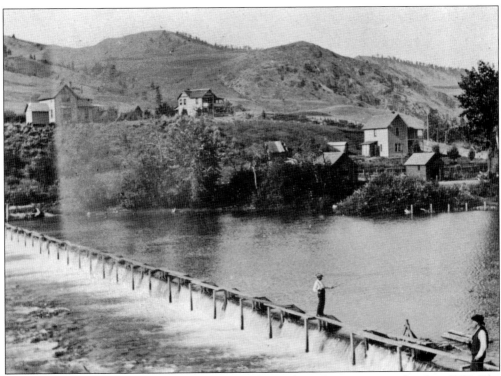

The first dam on the Chelan River, known as the Buckner Dam, was completed in 1892. The 5- to 6-foot-tall dam was built to provide water to south Chelan residents and better navigation in the Chelan area. After the original dam was washed out in 1893, it was rebuilt and was known as the Smith Dam. That dam was taken out by floods in 1894, along with the bridge.

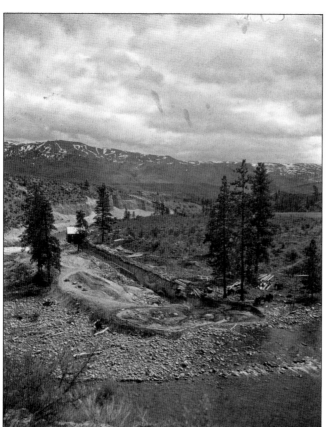

M. M. Kingman purchased the Chelan Water Power Company in 1899 and built a dam mainly for power generation. Electricity produced at the dam was delivered to Chelan in May 1903.

J. A. Larrabee is sitting in the foreground of this photograph of the breakwater at Chelan taken in 1903.

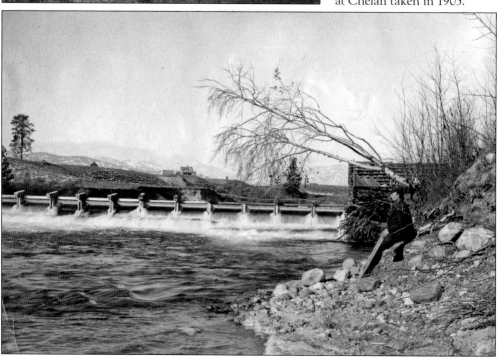

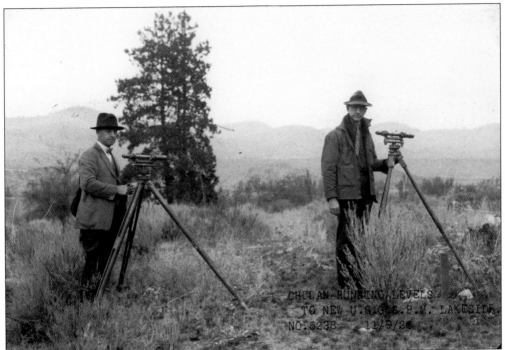

In 1925, the Washington Water Power Company purchased the Chelan Electric Company, which had purchased the Chelan Water Power Company in 1906. Shortly after, the company received a license to construct a new dam and powerhouse at Lake Chelan. The new dam would raise the lake level to 1,100 feet, 21 feet above the level at the time. Surveyors worked not only at the construction site, but also around the lake locating the contour line that would be the new lake level. Here the surveyors are at work at Lakeside on November 9, 1926. (Courtesy of the Chelan County PUD.)

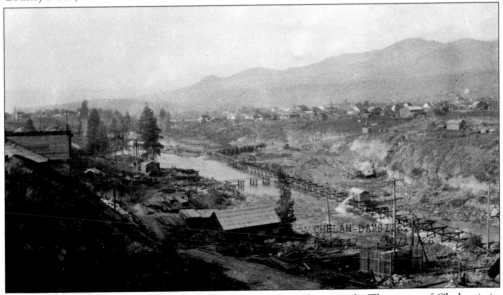

The site for the new dam is shown in this January 1926 photograph. The town of Chelan is in the background. (Courtesy of the Chelan County PUD.)

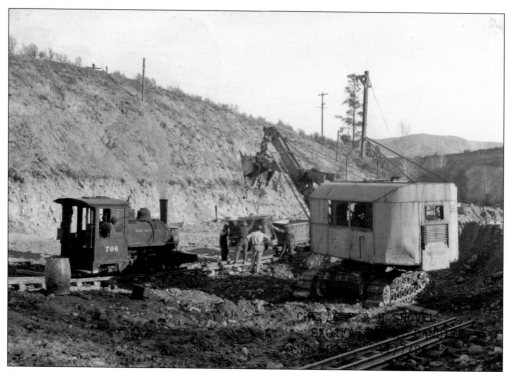

A narrow-gauge steam engine and hopper cars were used to remove rock and soil during the excavation of the dam site. (Courtesy of the Chelan County PUD.)

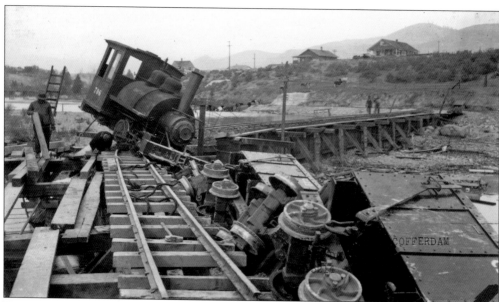

Engine 706 and several hopper cars derailed at the cofferdam in November 1926. (Courtesy of the Chelan County PUD.)

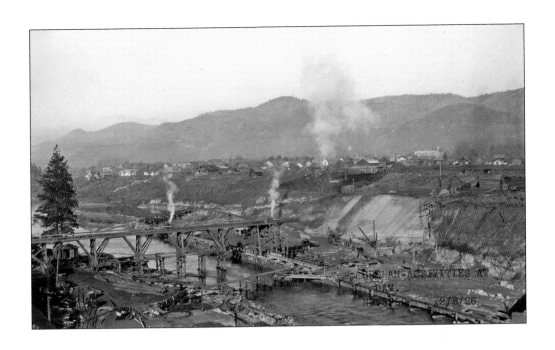

The dam's wood trestle structure took shape above the site during the winter of 1926–1927. (Both courtesy of the Chelan County PUD.)

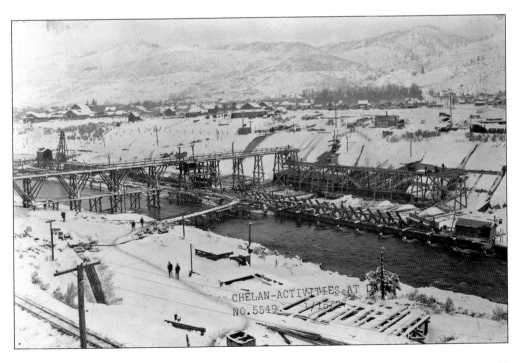

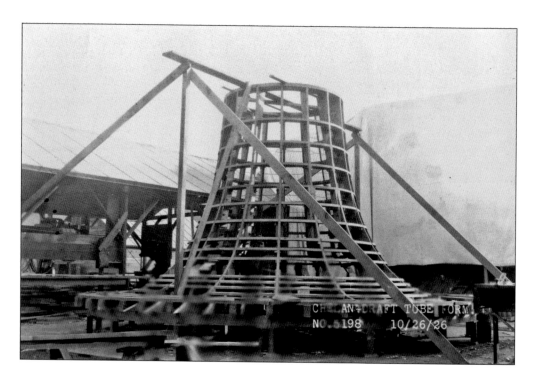

The forms that were built for the draft tube, which controls the flow of water as it exits the turbine, were a construction marvel themselves.

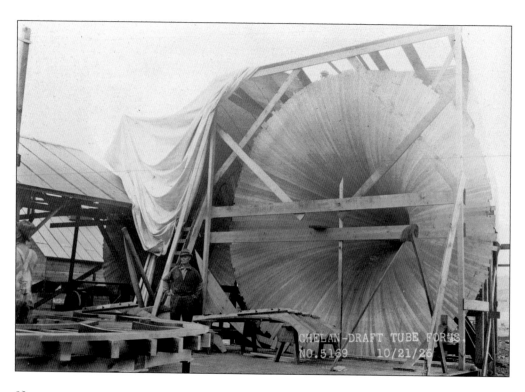

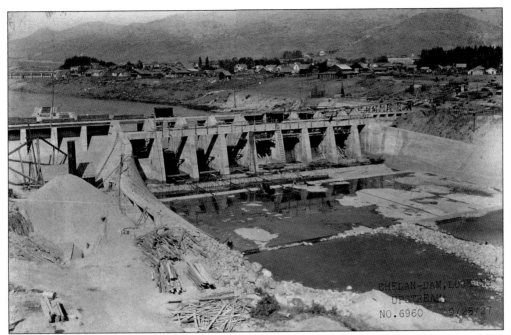

The Chelan Dam regulates the surface level of Lake Chelan and keeps the levels between 1,079 and 1,100 feet. This photograph was taken looking upstream toward Chelan on September 25, 1927. (Courtesy of the Chelan County PUD.)

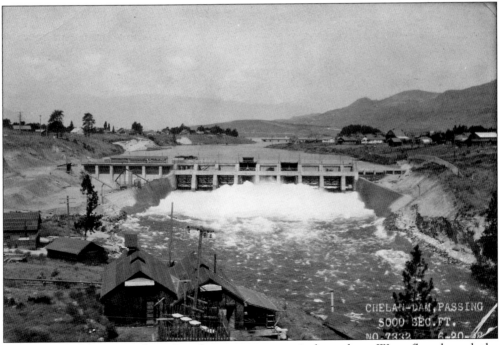

The completed dam, a steel-reinforced gravity structure, is shown here. Water flow through the dam was 5,000 cubic feet per second when this photograph was taken June 20, 1928. (Courtesy of the Chelan County PUD.)

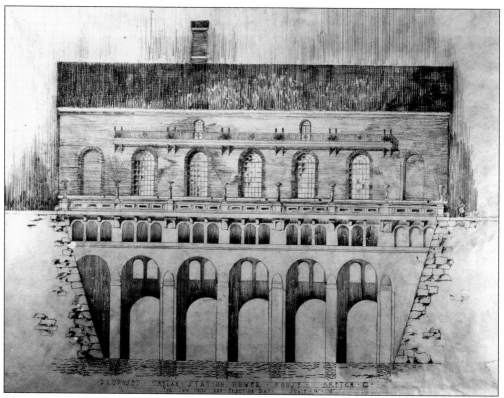

The ornate design of the powerhouse is shown in this architectural drawing. (Courtesy of the Chelan County PUD.)

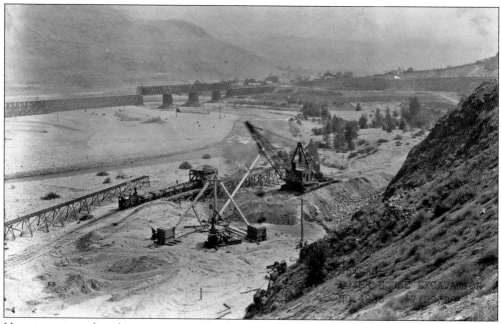

Here is a view of workers excavating for the powerhouse building. (Courtesy of the Chelan County PUD.)

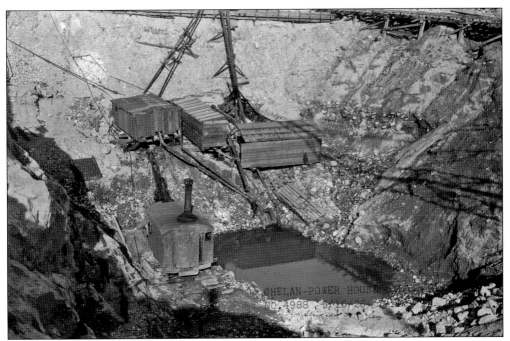

As the dam was built upstream, construction of the powerhouse started. (Courtesy of the Chelan County PUD.)

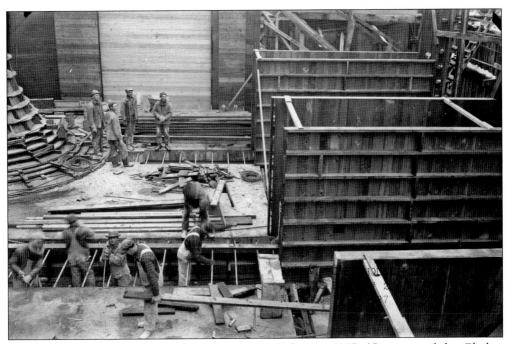

Forms were placed for the powerhouse piers in February 1927. (Courtesy of the Chelan County PUD.)

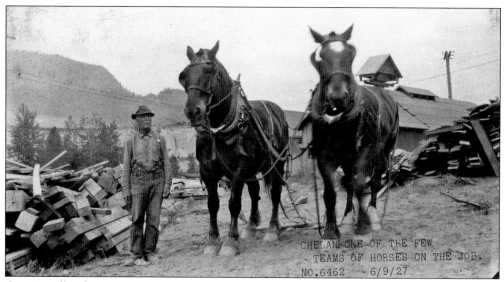

Occasionally a horse team worked on the job. (Courtesy of the Chelan County PUD.)

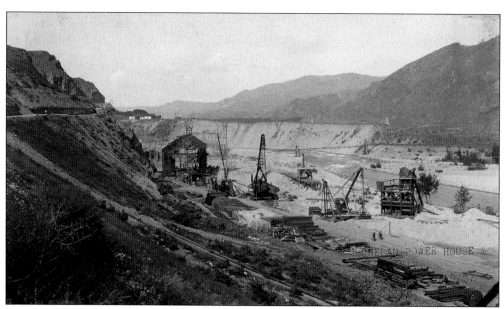

Construction of the powerhouse made progress during 1927. (Courtesy of the Chelan County PUD.)

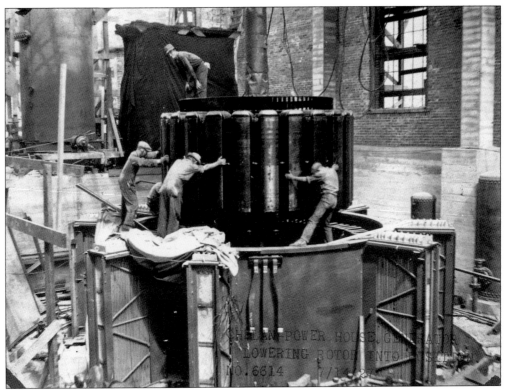

Workers at the powerhouse generator lower a rotor into position on July 14, 1927. (Courtesy of the Chelan County PUD.)

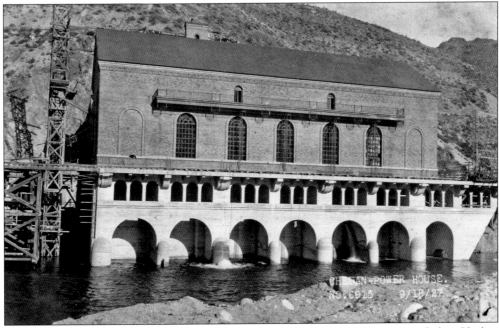

By September 1927, the powerhouse was near completion. (Courtesy of the Chelan County PUD.)

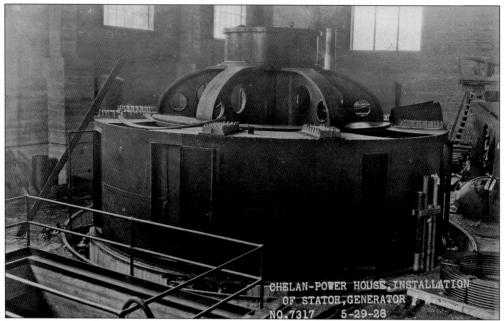

By August 1929, the powerhouse was complete. Shown here is one of the generators. (Courtesy of the Chelan County PUD.)

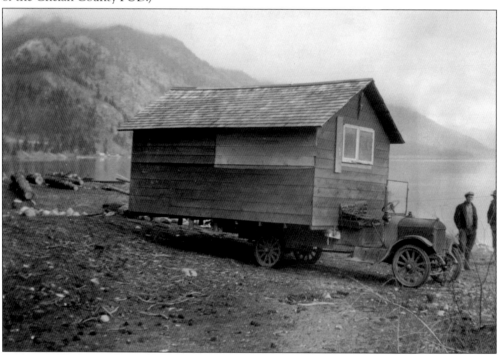

When Washington Water Power raised the level of Lake Chelan to the 1,100-foot level from 1,077 feet, many homes and outbuildings had to be moved to higher ground. Harold and Elizabeth Watson of First Creek lost their garden and part of the orchard. Also flooded were the camping grounds that had become their livelihood. To prepare the Watson home for the move, the kitchen section was separated from the rest of the house. (Courtesy of Elizabeth Watson Perry.)

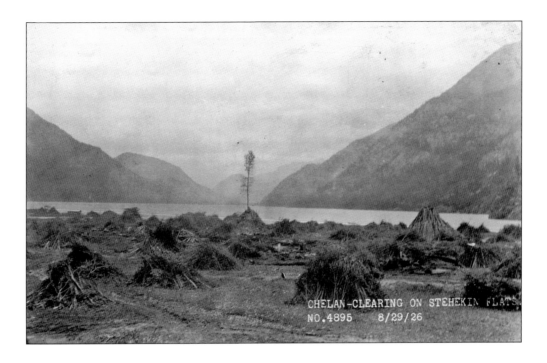

Clearing took place at Stehekin Flats as well. At the peak employment level, the dam construction employed 1,250 men. One thousand of these worked directly on the dam, tunnel, or powerhouse, and 250 cleared the lakeshore up to the new lake level. (Both courtesy of the Chelan County PUD.)

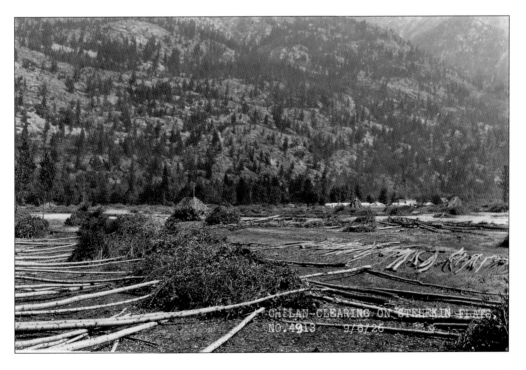

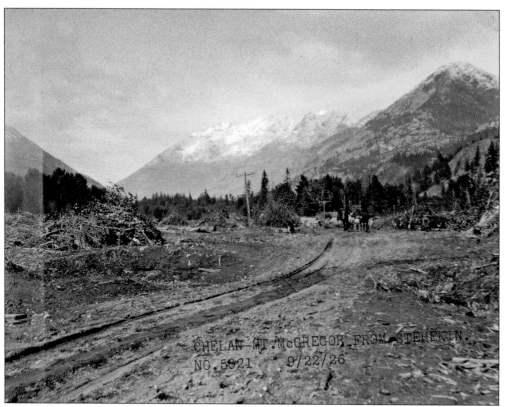

The workers clearing Stehekin Flats experienced the spectacular views, such as this view of Mount McGregor in the distance. (Courtesy of the Chelan County PUD.)

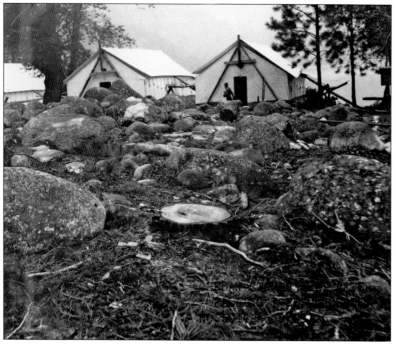

Before the lake level was raised, the timber was harvested in the areas to be flooded. Here, in September 1926, the stumps remaining near Lucerne are shown with the loggers' camp in the background. (Courtesy of the Chelan County PUD.)

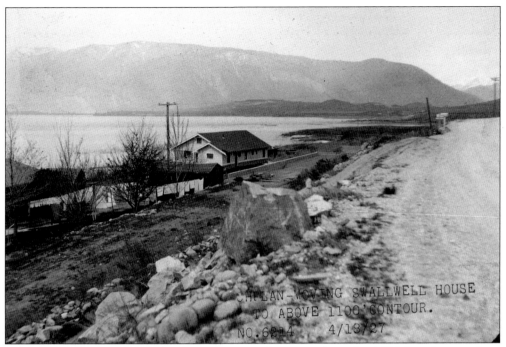

Here the Swallwell house is being moved to a new location, above the 1,100-foot elevation line, on April 18, 1927. (Courtesy of the Chelan County PUD.)

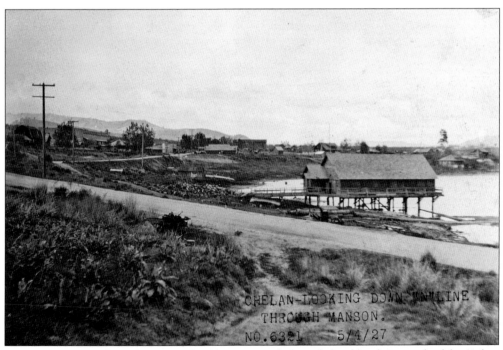

Manson lost its pavilion plus a considerable amount of relatively level land as a result of the 21-foot rise in the level of Lake Chelan. (Courtesy of the Chelan County PUD.)

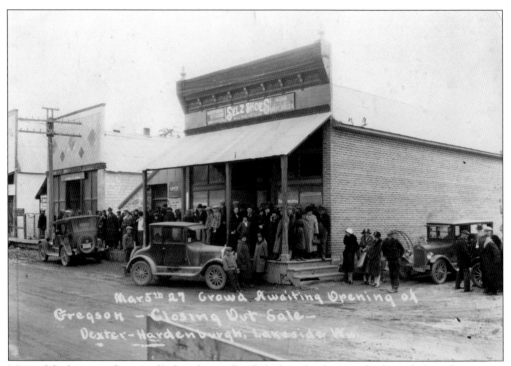

Most of the business district of Lakeside was flooded when the dam was built, including the Dexter-Hardenburgh store. On March 5, 1927, this eager crowd awaited the start of a closing-out sale at the store. In a photograph taken in earlier days, (from left to right) Ray Dexter, Elton Dexter, an unidentified man, and Joe Hardenburgh are shown inside the store.

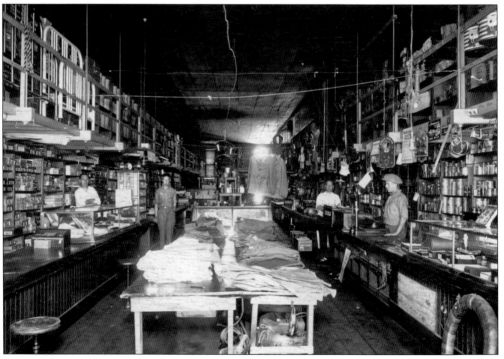

Eight

THE UPLAKE COMMUNITIES
LUCERNE, HOLDEN, AND MOORE'S POINT

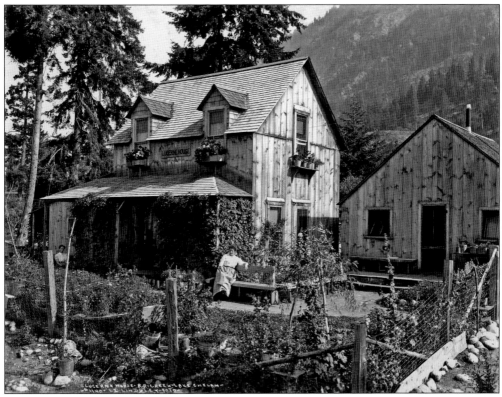

When railroad construction to mining claims up Railroad Creek started in 1901, Barbara Shearer, a native of Switzerland, opened a boardinghouse—the Lucerne House—at the lake. She had previously operated a boardinghouse on Bridge Creek and had also been a cook on the *Lady of the Lake*. In 1903, she was named postmaster of the new Lucerne Post Office, which was located in the corner of the boardinghouse. (University of Washington Libraries Special Collections, LIN0258.)

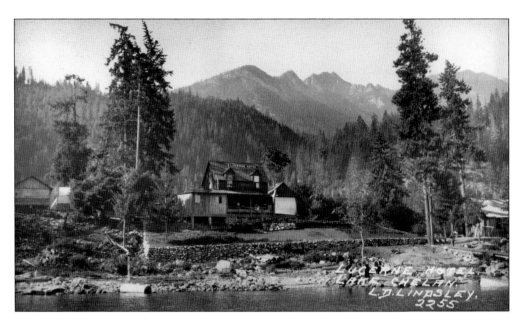

Under Barbara Shearer's ownership, the Lucerne House expanded so that by 1910 the hotel property included three buildings, three rowboats, and two launches. Steamers made regular stops at the Lucerne dock, which served Lucerne, Domke Lake, and the mining areas up Railroad Creek. Domke Lake, which was stocked with rainbow trout and steelhead by early resident A. L. Cool, was reachable by trail from Lucerne. Gordon Stuart, a true mountain man, continued to live at Domke Lake, trapping in the winter and hosting fishermen in the summer, until his death in 1985. Besides the post office, Lucerne offered an opportunity for socializing among the local residents in the form of a tavern, built in the 1920s. (Below, University of Washington Libraries Special Collections, WAS0154.)

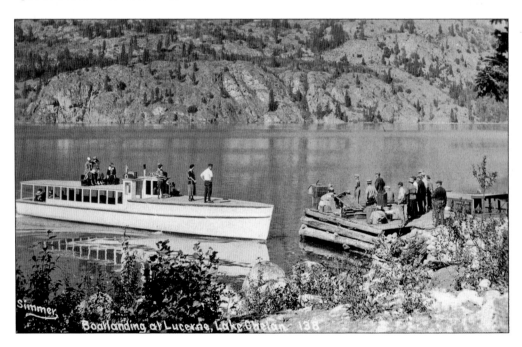

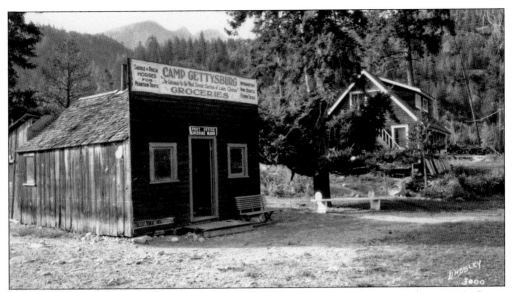

Barbara Shearer sold the Lucerne Hotel to Henry Kingman and Robert Little in 1913. Oscar Getty became postmaster in 1923 and moved the post office to a small building he named "Camp Gettysburg" on his property, which was adjacent to the Lucerne Hotel. The Lucerne Post Office was discontinued in 1956. (From the Byrd Collection; courtesy of Dennis King.)

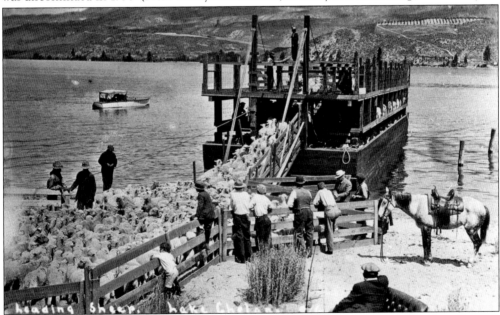

In 1915, the Lake Chelan Transportation Company, run by E. E. Shotwell and Roy Barton, completed construction of the barge *Blackfoot*, which was to be used to haul sheep to and from summer grazing areas. The *Blackfoot*, with three decks, could hold 2,400 sheep. Tom Drumheller wintered his sheep near Ephrata, Washington. In the spring, he herded them to the Columbia River across from Chelan Falls, ferried the herd across, and then herded the sheep to Lakeside, where they boarded the barge, bound for the meadows up-lake along the Chelan-Methow ridge. During the summer, the fatter lambs were loaded on railroad cars at Chelan Falls for shipment to Chicago.

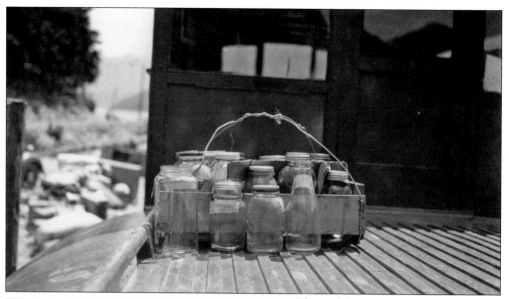

The up-lake communities were highly dependent on the lake steamers for delivering supplies and food, such as the fresh milk shown here. For milk deliveries, each bottle had the customer's name on it. The boat company kept the milk covered by ice and tarps.

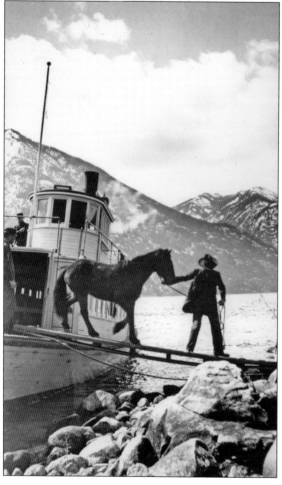

It was common to see passengers boarding or disembarking the steamers accompanied by their horses. Pack horses used in the upper valley in the summer often were moved by ferry to locations on other parts of the lake for the winter.

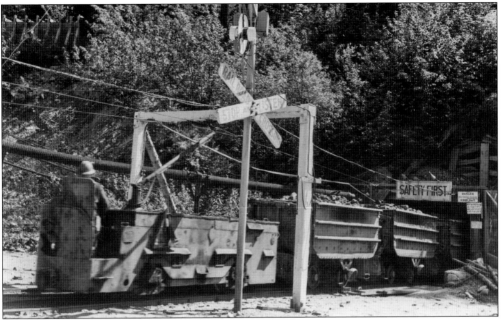

James Henry "Harry" Holden located four mining claims in the Railroad Creek Valley on July 24, 1896, while hunting grouse for lunch. By June 1900, he was the sole proprietor of the Holden Gold and Copper Mining Company and had plans to build a railroad from Refrigerator Harbor, just up-lake from Lucerne, to the mine. By the end of 1901, stockholder financing had run out and the Holden mine consisted of several tunnels, ore dumps, thousands of railroad ties, and several bridges. Howe Sound Mining Company of New York leased the property with the option to buy in August 1928. Beginning in 1937, with rising copper prices, Howe Sound began to invest significantly in development of the mine. By 1939, the company town of Holden was complete, with buildings to house 450 workers and their families, a hospital, a movie theater, and a school. These photographs of the operation were taken in the 1950s as the mine was nearing the end of production.

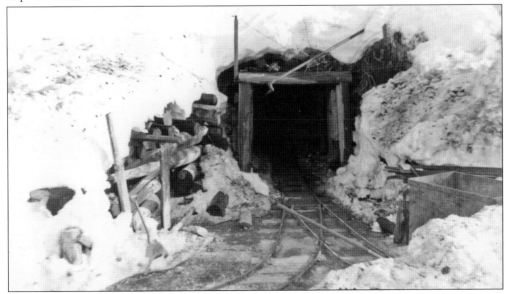

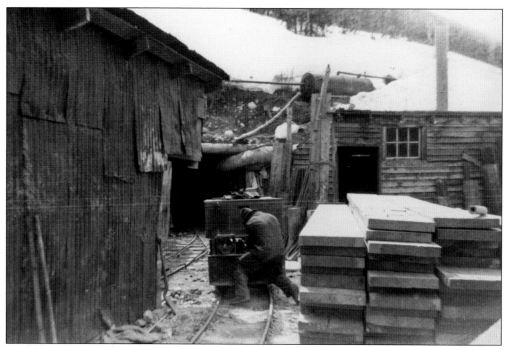

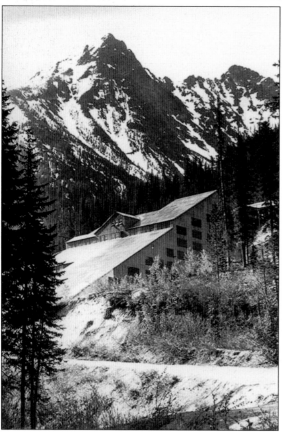

The first load—200 tons—of copper, gold, and zinc concentrates from the Holden mine was shipped from Holden by barge on April 7, 1938. Dignitaries from towns across north central Washington were invited to tour the mine and accompany the shipment to Chelan on boats escorting the tug *E. B. Schley* as it pushed the barges down-lake. Two days later, as the barges arrived in Chelan, there was a second celebration hosted by Chelan mayor William T. Price and the chamber of commerce. The high school band played, businesses closed, and several people addressed the crowd that had gathered. The crowd then followed by car as the truckloads of concentrate made their way to Chelan Falls for the journey to a Tacoma smelter.

Prof. Edward Lange, an artist from Seattle, sketched the Holden Mine operation.

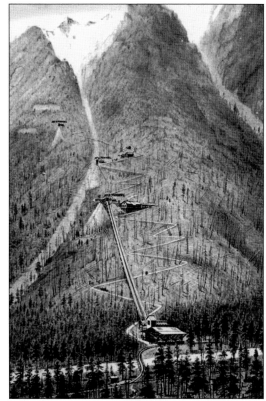

Howe Sound School District was established in Holden by the company after several families requested that they be included in the Chelan School District. A school (the Holden School) offering grades one through eight was built in the town. Children of Holden families attended high school away from home and returned to Holden during school breaks and summers.

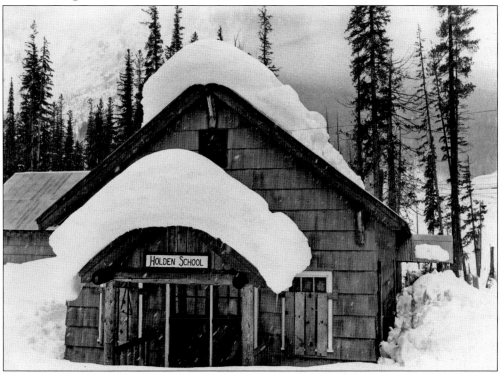

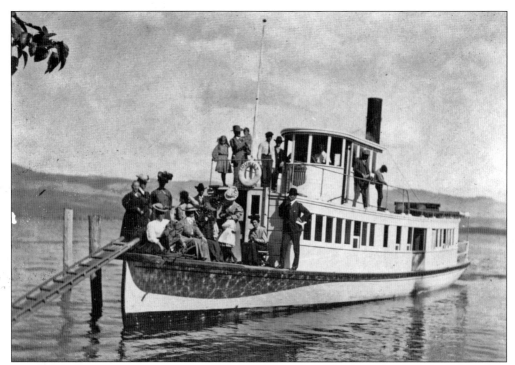

The *Tourist* served the up-lake communities in many ways, including carrying passengers, mail, and freight. Other duties included hauling apples for orchardists, hauling explosives for miners, and pulling barges loaded with horses.

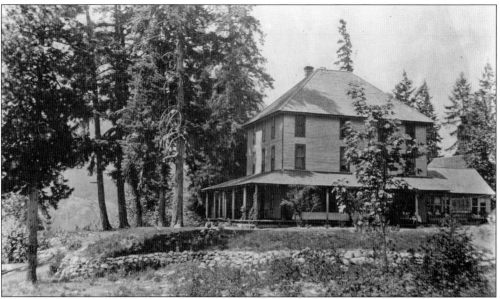

Mary Moore and her children Archibald ("Archie") and Mary ("Mamie") joined her husband, John R. Moore, at his Fish Creek claim in October 1890 and were surprised to find that there was only a tent for them to stay in. They built a home and began to take in boarders. Over the next few years, they built large additions to the original house, which became Moore's Hotel. It operated from 1892 until Mary's death in 1910.

Mary Moore is shown here with her son Archie.

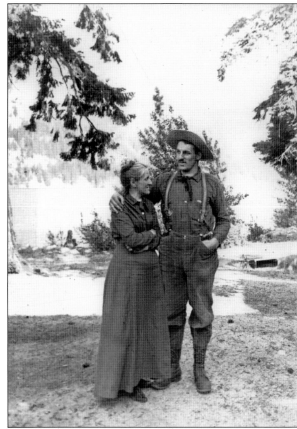

Hunters and trappers successfully worked the upper Stehekin Valley well into the 20th century. Here Tom Dodge and Hugh Courtney haul out a bear killed in the Moore's Point area in 1910. Meals at Moore's Hotel occasionally featured bear or goat.

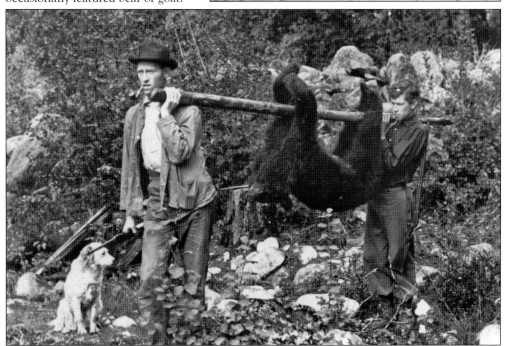

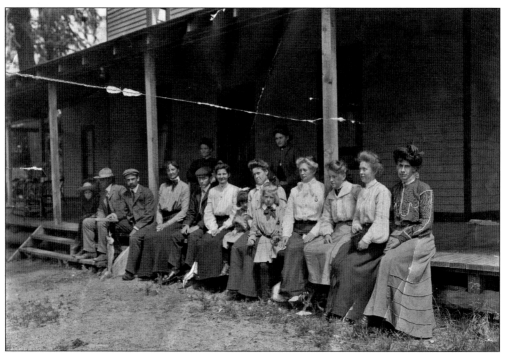

Mollie Kingman and daughter Melissa sit on the porch of Moore's Hotel behind a group of guests. Her son Lawrence and her husband, Herbert (holding a fish), sit on the steps in this photograph taken about 1900.

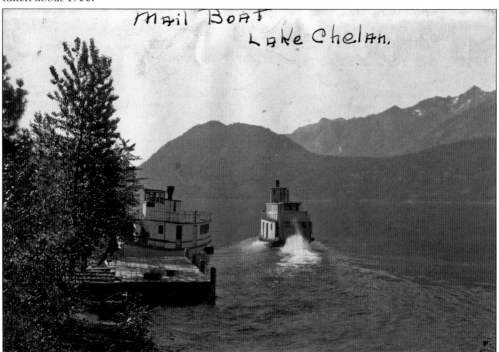

At one of the many docks up-lake, the *Swan* sits at the dock while the mail boat *Comet* heads for the next stop.

Nine

STEHEKIN

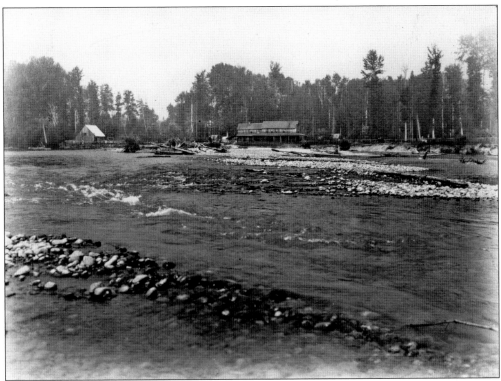

The Stehekin River Valley first attracted miners, who came to the area in large numbers shortly after George and John Rouse discovered deposits of gold, silver, and lead at Doubtful Lake in 1886. The easiest access to the Stehekin mining district was by lake, and Stehekin was the logical location of a mining base camp. The best land for homesteads was up the Stehekin Valley, where Maj. John W. Horton was the first to build a home site. Horton invited his son-in-law, George Hall, to the area. Hall, along with his wife, Georgia, and four children, arrived in 1889 and built a house and a two-story hotel called the Argonaut.

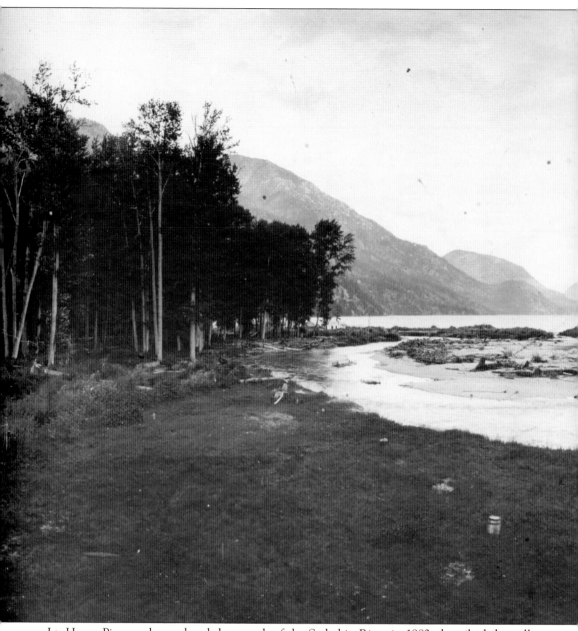

Lt. Henry Pierce, who explored the mouth of the Stehekin River in 1882, described the valley bottom as "dense jungle of cottonwood, willows, firs, and underbrush with frequent lagoons covered

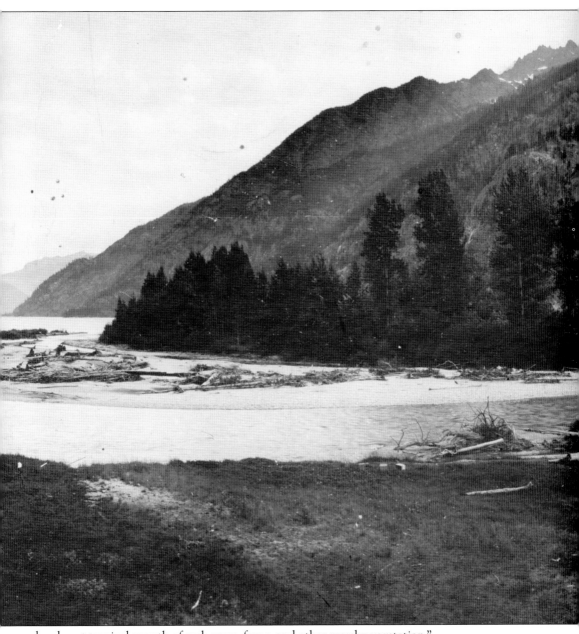

by almost tropical growth of rush grass, ferns, and other marshy vegetation."

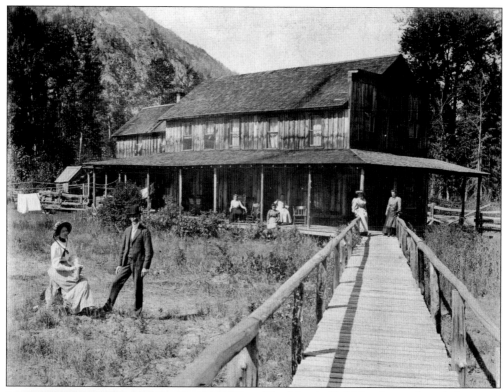

The Merritt Field family purchased the Argonaut from George Hall in 1892, and the hotel became known as the Field Hotel.

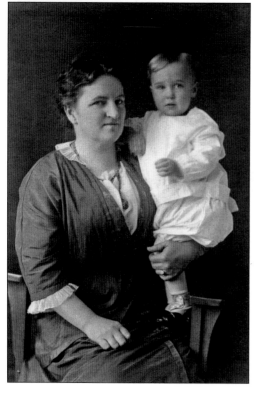

Martha Field and her son Walter are shown in this 1915 portrait.

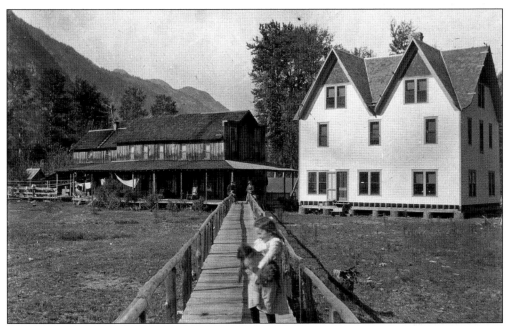

Olive Field, Merritt and Martha's daughter, posed in front of the family's newly expanded hotel in this 1900 photograph. Olive later married Harry Buckner, and they made their home at the Buckner homestead, which Harry's parents (William Van and May) had purchased from William Buzzard in 1910. The Buckner homestead today is a part of the Lake Chelan National Recreation Area and is preserved as an example of early homesteading efforts in the valley.

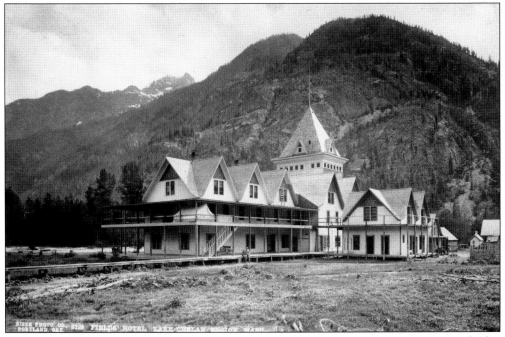

The Field Hotel had 25 guest rooms, and the complex included a laundry room, a wagon shed, a barn, and a cellar. After logging part of the property, there were 100 acres of pasture and cropland on the property, allowing for local hay, fruit, and vegetable production.

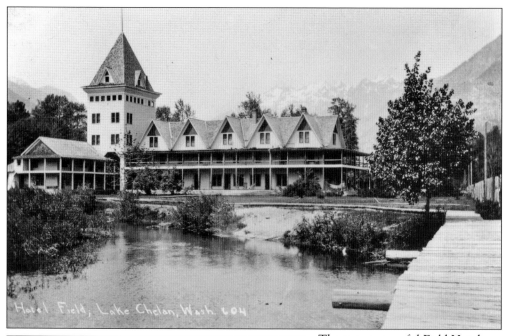

Hotel Field, Lake Chelan, Wash. 604

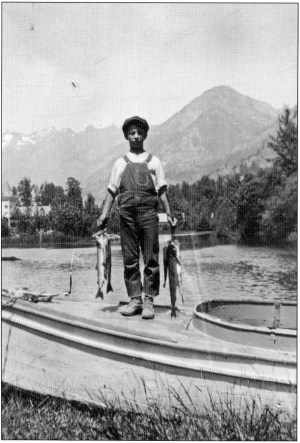

The very successful Field Hotel expanded in 1905 to include an impressive, large structure that could host 100 guests per night. All guests could enjoy fine food along with access to services that included boating, backcountry guide services, and pack trains. The Great Northern Railroad purchased the hotel in 1915. An Easterner could purchase a single ticket that included rail fare to Wenatchee, riverboat fare to Chelan Falls, a stagecoach to the lake, and steamboat fare to Stehekin.

Ab Garton is shown with his catch of the day in this photograph dated 1915 or 1916.

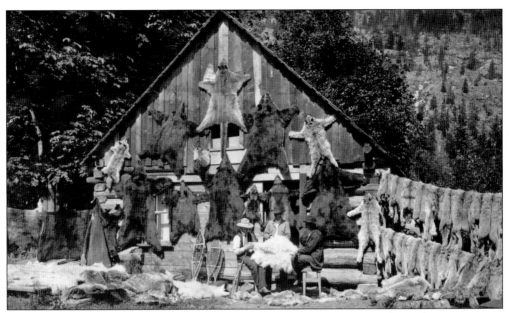

Lewis and James Weaver arrived in Stehekin in 1903, hoping to support themselves as trappers. They established a taxidermy business in Stehekin, where they displayed their fur rugs and robes both inside and outside their store. Their customers included hunters, who wanted to take a souvenir of their trip home, as well as tourists visiting the area. James died during the 1908–1909 trapping season. Lewis sold the business and moved down-lake until 1913, when he returned to Stehekin with his wife, Daisy. They homesteaded 85 acres in the area now known as Weaver Point. They supplied the Field Hotel with fresh milk and vegetables. The Weaver Brothers' Store is shown here. The interior photograph was taken on July 19, 1909.

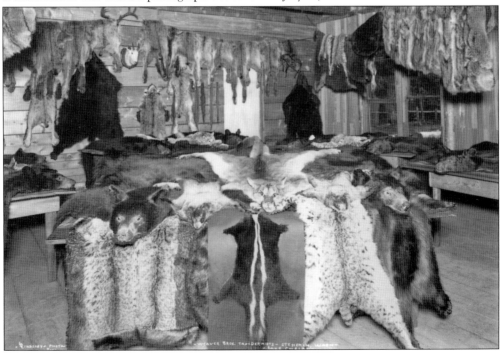

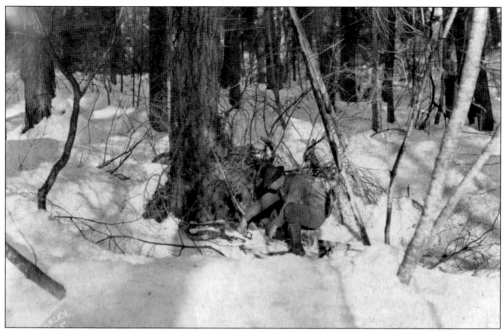

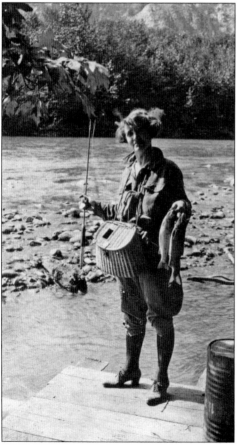

Sherman Pearl arrived at Lake Chelan in 1890 and homesteaded at Hazzard Creek, on the north shore of the lake near Stehekin. His claim was validated just hours before the U.S. Forest Service took over the remaining forest lands of the area. He was a carpenter, and he also had mining claims near his homestead. Here he is shown trapping near Stehekin in 1908.

A recreational fisherwoman displays her catch on September 11, 1925.

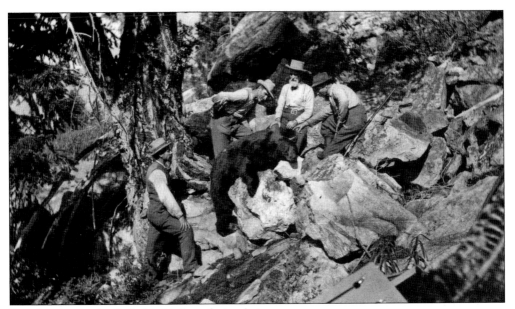

Bear hunters in the Stehekin Valley admire their success.

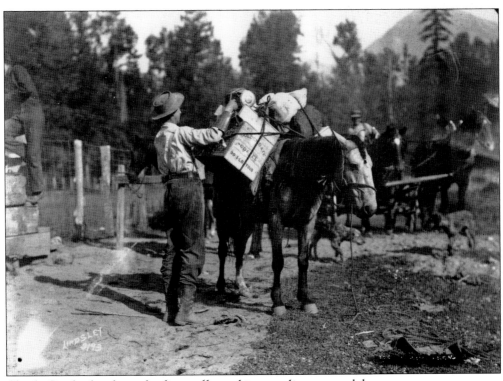

Claude Graybeal is shown loading coffee-making supplies on a pack horse.

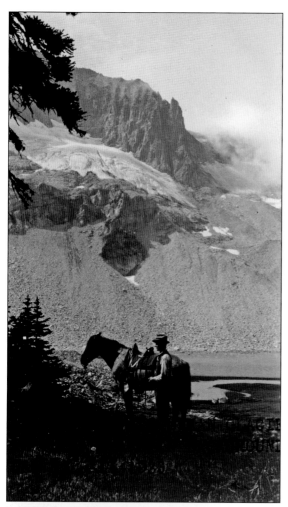

After the Chelan dam was constructed in 1927, the Washington Water Power Company built huts at several locations. Crews used the huts when they were sent on the annual snow survey—a series of snow depth measurements—throughout the Lake Chelan drainage, which were used to project runoff during spring snowmelt. Gordon Stuart often contracted to do this survey. Here one of the snow survey workers and his horse are shown with Lyman Lake in background. (Courtesy of the Chelan County PUD.)

Mr. Pershall, Mrs. Pershall, Sarah Wood, and Tom and Nell Johnson take a hike at Horseshoe Basin in the early 1900s.

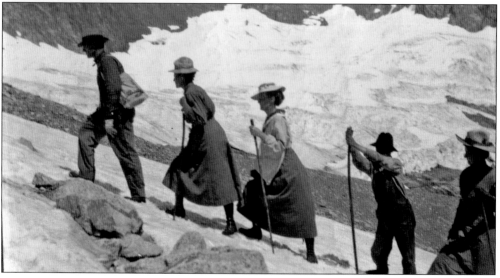

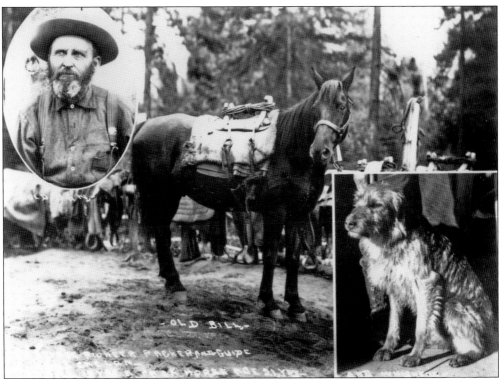

- OLD BILL -

Dan Devore moved to the Stehekin area in 1889 and became well known as a packer, leading pack trains to mining camps and leading tourists on backcountry tours. In 1916, he led author Mary Roberts Rinehart, her sons, and a crew from the Great Northern Railroad up the Stehekin Valley. Rinehart published her account of the trip in the book *Tenting To-Night*. Devore's horse, Old Bill, and his dog Whiskers were mentioned in the book.

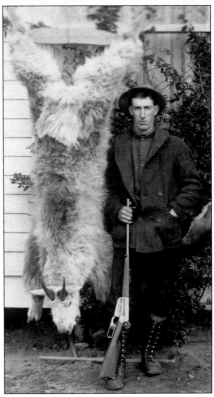

Mountain goats were abundant in the valley in the early years. Henry Domke once promised to repay a debt to the proprietors of the Woodin-Nichols sawmill with a treat of "venison." Christopher Robinson related the rest of the story: "The venison came in the course of time, but it looked different than any I had ever seen. It was a big, fine hindquarter, with a cloven hoof, alright. But the hair on the shank was white. Charles Woodin was acting as chef for a bunch of hungry sawmill hands, so he cut off a generous supply of fine steaks, filled a couple of frying pans, got some of the meat turned over in the pan and then found that he could not get the fork into the meat again. The longer it cooked the harder it got. . . . it evidently was billy goat meat."

123

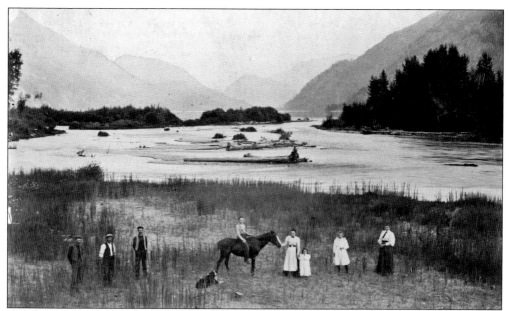

The course of the Stehekin River at its mouth was ever-changing. Here a group of visitors to Stehekin Flats poses with the spectacular panorama of the Lake Chelan Valley as a backdrop.

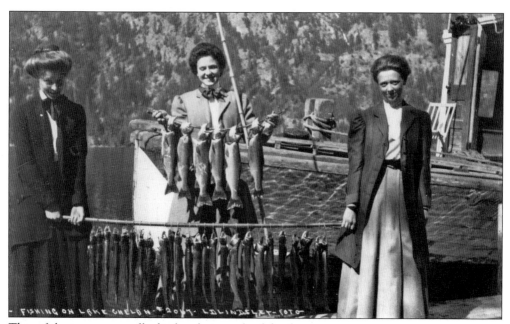

Three fisherwomen proudly display their catch of the day.

124

L. D. Lindsley was the grandson of the early Seattle resident David Denny. He was known as a miner, hunter, guide, and naturalist, as well as a photographer. Between 1910 and 1914, he lived in the Lake Chelan Valley, in a home owned by his parents, and worked as a photographer for the Great Northern Railroad. He was the character "Silent Lawrie" in Mary Roberts Rinehart's book *Tenting To-Night*. Not only did he take spectacular photographs of the area, he also carefully documented them. Here he is shown at work in the Agnes Creek Valley.

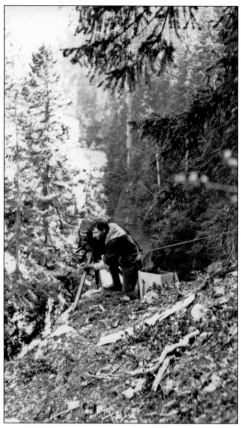

In 1893, sixteen-year-old Nellie Little traveled to Horseshoe Basin and made an entry in her diary describing the experience: "We came around a curve on the mountain side, and stood, speechless, and gazed at the glorious sight ahead of us! We were only about a mile from where we were to stop, and now we could see so plainly, the grand and wonderful Horseshoe Basin. O, will I ever forget that grandest of all views? I had been enraptured with the fine scenery, getting more grand as we went up, all the way, but when I saw Horseshoe Basin, my wonder and admiration knew no bounds!"

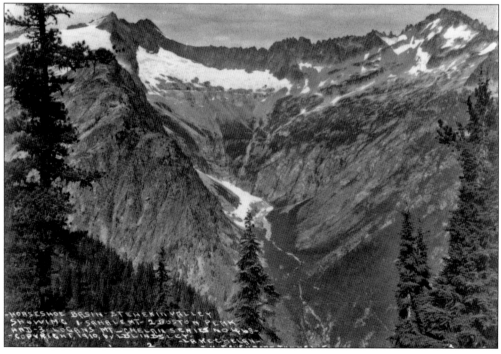

BIBLIOGRAPHY

Adams, Nigel B. *The Holden Mine: Discovery to Production, 1896–1938*. Wenatchee, WA: Published for the Washington State Historical Society by the World Publishing Company, 1981.

Bryant, Sandy K. Nelson. *Mountain Air: The Life of Gordon Stuart—Mountain Man of the North Cascades*. Wenatchee, WA: Directed Media, Inc., 1986.

Buckner Homestead Historic District. Seattle: Northwest Interpretive Association in cooperation with North Cascades National Park Service Complex, 1998.

Byrd, Robert. *Lake Chelan in the 1890s*. Wenatchee, WA: Byrd-Song Publishing, 1992.

Darvill, Fred T. Jr. *Stehekin—A Guide to the Enchanted Valley*. Edmonds, WA: Signpost Books, 1981.

Hackenmiller, T. *Ladies of the Lake*. Wenatchee, WA: Point Publishing, 1998.

———. *Wapato Heritage: The History of the Chelan and Entiat Indians*. Wenatchee, WA: Point Publishing, 1995.

Lake Chelan History Notes. Volumes I (1973)–XXIII (2008). Chelan, WA: Lake Chelan Historical Society.

Linsley, Daniel C. "A Railroad Survey Across the North Cascades in 1870." *Northwest Discovery: The Journal of Northwest History and Natural History* 2 (April 1981).

McConnell, Grant. *Stehekin, A Valley in Time*. Seattle: The Mountaineers, 1988.

Northwest Underground Explorations. *Discovering Washington's Historic Mines, Volume 2: The East Central Cascade Mountains and the Wenatchee Mountains*. Arlington, WA: Oso Publishing Company, 2002.

Ray, Verne F. "Ethnohistorical Notes on the Columbia, Chelan, Entiat, and Wenatchee Tribes." from David Agee Horr's *American Indian Ethnohistory: Indians of the Northwest*. New York: Garland Publishing, Inc., 1974.

Rinehart, Mary Roberts. *Tenting To-Night*. Helena, MT: Riverbend Publishing in cooperation with the Montana Historical Society, 2002 (originally published 1918).

Scheuerman, Richard. *The Wenatchee Valley and Its First Peoples*. Walla Walla, WA: Color Press, 2005.

Stanford, Wayne. *Glimpses of Manson History*. Manson, WA: Frontier Publishing, 1993.

Wapato, Paul Grant. "Paschal Sherman: A life of accomplishment and service." *Tribal Tribune*, www.tribune.colvilletribes.com/archives/2005/june2005/reservation_paschalsherman.htm.

About the Lake Chelan Historical Society

The Lake Chelan Historical Society was organized in 1970 as an educational nonprofit charitable organization. It operates a historical museum in Chelan in the old Miners and Merchants Bank Building donated by Seattle-First National Bank.

All are invited to join the Lake Chelan Historical Society. As a member, you will receive the yearly edition of *History Notes*, and with a Life Membership, your name will be added to the Wall of Fame at the museum.

Lake Chelan Historical Society
204 East Woodin Avenue
P.O. Box 1498
Chelan, WA 98816
509-682-5644
www.chelanmuseum.com
E-mail: museum@chelanmuseum.com

ACROSS AMERICA, PEOPLE ARE DISCOVERING
SOMETHING WONDERFUL. THEIR HERITAGE.

Arcadia Publishing is the leading local history publisher in the United States. With more than 5,000 titles in print and hundreds of new titles released every year, Arcadia has extensive specialized experience chronicling the history of communities and celebrating America's hidden stories, bringing to life the people, places, and events from the past. To discover the history of other communities across the nation, please visit:

www.arcadiapublishing.com

Customized search tools allow you to find regional history books about the town where you grew up, the cities where your friends and family live, the town where your parents met, or even that retirement spot you've been dreaming about.

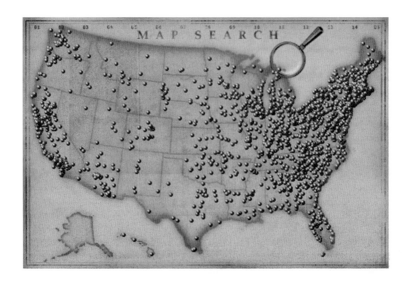